Grade
5

Summer Study
Daily Activity Workbook

Written by **Christine Hood**

Illustrations by **Judy Stead**

New York

New York

An Imprint of Sterling Publishing
387 Park Avenue South
New York, NY 10016

ISBN 978-1-4114-6538-1

Distributed in Canada by Sterling Publishing
c/o Canadian Manda Group, 165 Dufferin Street
Toronto, Ontario, Canada M6K 3H6
Distributed in the United Kingdom by GMC Distribution Services
Castle Place, 166 High Street, Lewes, East Sussex, England BN7 1XU
Distributed in Australia by Capricorn Link (Australia) Pty. Ltd.
P.O. Box 704, Windsor, NSW 2756, Australia

For information about custom editions, special sales, and premium and corporate purchases, please
contact Sterling Special Sales at 800-805-5489 or specialsales@sterlingpublishing.com.

Manufactured in Canada
Lot #:
2 4 6 8 10 9 7 5 3
07/12

www.flashkids.com

Cover design and production by Mada Design, Inc.

DEAR PARENT,

As a parent, you want your child to have time to relax and have fun during the summer, but you don't want your child's math and reading skills to get rusty. How do you make time for summer fun and also ensure that your child will be ready for the next school year?

This *Summer Skills Daily Activity Workbook* provides short, fun activities in reading and math to help children keep their skills fresh all summer long. This book not only reviews what children learned during fourth grade, it also introduces what they'll be learning in fifth grade. The numbered daily activities make it easy for children to complete one activity a day and stay on track the whole summer long. Best of all, the games, puzzles, and stories help children retain their knowledge as well as build new skills. By the time your child finishes the book, he or she will be ready for a smooth transition into fifth grade.

As your child completes the activities in this book, shower him or her with encouragement and praise. You can feel good knowing that you are taking an active and important role in your child's education. Helping your child complete the activities in this book is providing him or her with an excellent example—that you value learning, every day! Have a wonderful summer, and most of all, have fun learning together!

PREPOSITION POEM

A **preposition** is a word that indicates direction, time, and location of nouns and pronouns. Read this preposition poem. Underline the prepositions. The first one is done for you.

Out the door,
Down the street,
Around the corner,
Onto the bus,
Into my seat,
Off the bus,
Over the playground,
Into my classroom,
School!

Now, write your own preposition poem! Choose a topic that includes lots of action, like playing a sport or making a meal. The last line should summarize or tell the topic. Use as many different prepositions as you can. Use the words in the box to help you.

about	above	across	after	around	at	before
below	beside	by	down	during	for	from
inside	into	of	off	on	out	outside
over	through	to	under	up	with	without

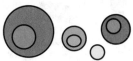

COUNTING CASH

Look at each money value shown in the chart. Use the least amount of bills and coins to make that value. The first one is done for you.

Value	5	1	25¢	10¢	5¢	1¢
$3.52	0	3	2	0	0	2
$6.23						
$4.78						
$8.92						
$7.03						
$5.16						
$9.44						
$2.65						
$8.90						
$4.86						
$3.99						
$9.67						

Answer each question. Write the least number of bills and coins received.

1. Josh's lunch was $7.27. He paid with two $5 bills. How much change did he get back?

_____

$1 bills _____ quarters _____ dimes _____ nickels _____ pennies _____

2. Anya bought trail mix and juice for $2.85. She paid with a $5 bill. How much change did she get back? _____

$1 bills _____ quarters _____ dimes _____ nickels _____ pennies _____

A VERY LOUD DAY

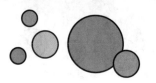

How many things would it take to make a very loud day?
Write the plural for each noun to find out.

1. 1 honking horn   4 honking   _____horns_____

2. 1 crying baby   2 crying   _____

3. 1 howling wolf   6 howling   _____

4. 1 tumbling box   10 tumbling   _____

5. 1 yelling man   5 yelling   _____

6. 1 buzzing fly   3 buzzing   _____

7. 1 squeaking mouse   7 squeaking   _____

8. 1 marching band   5 marching   _____

9. 1 giggling elf   10 giggling   _____

10. 1 ticking watch   20 ticking   _____

11. 1 screeching monkey   14 screeching   _____

12. 1 car crashing   12 crashing   _____

13. 1 breaking glass   8 breaking   _____

14. 1 bleating sheep   25 bleating   _____

15. 1 squealing child   40 squealing   _____

Day 5:
Plurals

3 X 3 MAGIC SQUARES

All rows and columns in these "magic" squares add up to the magic number.
Can you complete the magic squares? Hint: You can use a number only once!

1. All rows and columns add up to 14.

11		
3	7	
		9

2. All rows and columns add up to 16.

	2	
1		
	8	3

3. All rows and columns add up to 20.

10		
8		3
	5	

4. All rows and columns add up to 23.

		2
	12	5
	4	

5. All rows and columns add up to 32.

12		7
17		
		20

6. All rows and columns add up to 45.

	15	
		18
22	16	

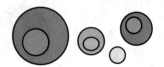
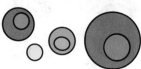

WHICH WORD?

Homophones are words that sound the same but have different meanings and spellings. Read the clues for each set of words. One of the words is in the word box. Write it next to the correct clue. Then write the homophones for the other clues.

fowl	flour	its	heel
meet	so	to	whether
do	wood	there	marry

1. Beef _____ meat _____

Get to know _____ meet _____

2. That place _____

They are _____

Belongs to them _____

3. Bird _____

Not fair _____

4. Milled grain _____

Bloom _____

5. Join together _____

Cheery _____

6. Belonging to it _____

It is _____

7. In order that _____

Mend _____

plant _____

8. If _____

Condition of air, temperature _____

9. Trunk of a tree _____

Willing to _____

10. Toward a place _____

Also _____

One plus one _____

11. Small _____

Moisture _____

Owed _____

12. Bottom of foot _____

Make well _____

He will _____

PRACTICE WITH FRACTIONS

Rewrite each fraction using numerals.

1. Six and seven-tenths. $6\frac{7}{10}$

2. Fourteen and two-thirds. _____

3. Nine and one-fifth. _____

4. Seventeen and eight-ninths. _____

Reduce each fraction.

5. $\frac{17}{4}$ = _____

6. $3\frac{21}{7}$ = _____

7. $8\frac{13}{10}$ = _____

8. $\frac{26}{5}$ = _____

9. $15\frac{10}{3}$ = _____

10. $4\frac{18}{4}$ = _____

Complete each number sentence using **>**, **<**, or **=**.

11. $6\frac{4}{5}$ ☐ $\frac{37}{6}$

12. $\frac{25}{5}$ ☐ $\frac{19}{4}$

13. $\frac{34}{8}$ ☐ $4\frac{1}{2}$

14. $\frac{18}{6}$ ☐ $\frac{12}{4}$

15. $7\frac{9}{3}$ ☐ $8\frac{12}{6}$

16. 5 ☐ $\frac{32}{7}$

PARTS OF SPEECH

Identify these parts of speech in each sentence: noun, adjective, verb, preposition, and article. Write **N** above the nouns, **ADJ** above the adjectives, **V** above the verbs, **P** above the prepositions, and **A** above the articles.

> **ADJ N V A ADJ N P A N**
> **Example:** Merry Mario made a mighty mess in the mud.

1. Wild Willy watched the wavy worms wiggle and wobble.
(ADJ N V A ADJ N V V)

2. Pretty Patty picked a pricey pink dress.

3. Oliver opened the oven to check on oily omelets.

4. Cheery Charlie chose chunky cheese to chew.

5. Harry the hippo helped Hanna hide huge holey hats.

6. Funny Frannie found flat flowers under the floor.

7. Bored Benny bought bundles of bright blue balloons.

8. Jessica Jones juggled jars of juicy jiggling jelly.

9. Crazy cats crooned and cried under the moon.

10. Dizzy Darryl drove his dusty dog in his dirty truck.

11. Lumpy, lounging lions laughed and licked lollipops.

12. A team of tired tigers tasted ten tangy tacos for a treat.

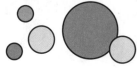

EARLY OR LATE?

Look at the time on each clock. Is the person early or late? Circle your answer.

1. Maya's dance class starts in 2 hours, 10 minutes. She got to class at 4:45.

EARLY   (LATE)

2. The Joneses will eat dinner in 1 hour, 30 minutes. Steven sat down to eat at 6:05.

EARLY   LATE

3. Open House is in 3 hours, 40 minutes. Melissa's parents got to the room at 7:20.

EARLY   LATE

4. Marcus walks the dog in 2 hours, 40 minutes. He will leave at 9:00.

EARLY   LATE

5. The softball game is in 4 hours, 20 minutes. Tham will take the field at 5:50.

EARLY   LATE

6. The talent show starts at 7:30. Leah will arrive in 2 hours, 15 minutes.

EARLY   LATE

7. School ends in 3 hours, 30 minutes. Dan's swim meet begins $\frac{1}{2}$ hour after school. Dan will get to the meet at 3:05.

EARLY   LATE

8. Morgan's shift begins in 4 hours, 20 minutes. She will get to work at 1:00 on the dot.

EARLY   LATE

9. The birthday party ends at 4:30. The party begins in 3 hours, 35 minutes. Jenny will get to the party at 12:45.

EARLY   LATE

10. Jack will get to baseball camp in $4\frac{1}{2}$ hours. Camp lasts for $6\frac{1}{2}$ hours. Camp ends at 6:45 PM.

EARLY   LATE

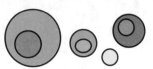 # GIANTS OF THE SEA

Read the article. Then answer the questions below.

There are about 75 different kinds of whales. They are the largest animals in the ocean. In fact, the blue whale is the largest animal in the world. Blue whales aren't really blue. They are more of a gray-blue with whitish speckles. A blue whale grows to about 80 feet long and weighs about 120 tons. Its heart is the size of a small car and weighs about 1,000 pounds. The blue whale is also the loudest animal on earth. Blue whales talk to each other through whistles. These whistles can reach levels up to 188 decibels and can be heard for hundreds of miles. The sound of a jet engine is only 140 decibels!

Blue whales are baleen whales. This means that they filter tiny plankton and fish from the water. They are called "gulpers" because they gulp mouthfuls of plankton or fish as they swim. Fifty to seventy throat pleats allow the throat to expand and form a large pouch. The water is then forced through the baleen plates hanging from the upper jaw. The baleen acts like a sieve catching the food. A blue whale will eat 2,000 to 9,000 pounds of plankton each day during the summer feeding season.

1. How many different kinds of whales are there? _____ *about 75* _____

2. How big does a blue whale grow to be? _____

3. How do blue whales talk to each other? _____

4. a blue whale louder than a lion? _____
How do you know?
_____
_____

5. What is a baleen whale?
_____
_____

6. Explain how a blue whale feeds.
_____
_____

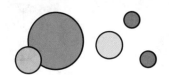
STARRY SKIES
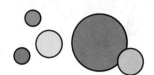

Multiply. Then circle the stars with the answers.

2	9	12	4	6	10
x 2	x 9	x 12	x 4	x 6	x 10

11	5	1	3	8	7
x 11	x 5	x 1	x 3	x 8	x 7

72   144   4   9   12   16   25   36

81   49   1   100   121   64   30   18

Troy

Tanya

Who counted the most stars? _____

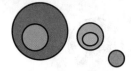

MAKE IT BETTER

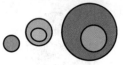

Read each simple sentence. Can you make the situation better? Turn each simple sentence into a compound sentence by adding a conjunction and another sentence part. Use the conjunctions in the box to help you. Remember to use a comma before a conjunction in a compound sentence.

Example: My bike is broken.
My bike is broken, but my dad is driving me to school.

Conjunctions

although   yet   and   but   or

1. I lost my backpack at the museum.

_____

2. My lunchbox is full of bugs.

_____

3. I dropped my homework in the mud.

_____

4. I ripped a hole in my jeans.

_____

5. My pet bird flew out of its cage.

_____

6. The class field trip is canceled.

_____

7. I spilled juice on my shirt.

_____

8. The puppy chewed up my shoes.

_____

9. Our team lost the game.

_____

10. I can't go out and play in the rain.

_____

ADDING AND SUBTRACTING DECIMALS

Add or subtract. If needed, use placeholders and borrow.

1. 26.7
+ 18.1
———
44.8

2. 93.6
– 2.9
———

3. 7.30
+ 19.6
———

4. 62.79
+ 3.15
———

5. 87.50
– 3.47
———

6. 42.55
– 1.7
———

7. 86.9
+ 10.25
———

8. 51.07
– 3.03
———

9. 4.67
+ 18.36
———

10. 27.5
+ 4.33
———

11. 37.88
– 26.04
———

12. 99.73
– 78.80
———

13. 69.9
+ 4.54
———

14. 46.77
– 42.93
———

15. 61.58
+ 9.33
———

16. 27.5
– 5.80
———

WHAT IS THE GENRE?

There are many different kinds of stories. These different types of stories are called **genres**.
Look at the genres in the box. Then read each passage below. Write the genre on the line.

> **Genres**
>
> fiction   nonfiction   fairy tale   myth   tall tale
>
> fable   biography   poetry   mystery   science fiction

1. Jorge is reading a book about the life of baseball player Jackie Robinson. He is learning about the struggles Robinson faced as the first African American to play in the major leagues. What genre is it?
_____**biography**_____

2. Alex is reading a story that has been passed down from long ago. This story tells how the ancient Greeks thought their gods made the seasons change. Alex's favorite god is Apollo, god of the sun. What genre is it? _____

3. Kate is reading a story about a princess who loses her magic sword. She's helped by a fairy who makes the princess realize she can fight the evil dragon with her own powers, without the sword. What genre is it? _____

4. Suri is reading a story about a famous TV pet that goes missing. When the owners find out that it's been kidnapped, they follow clues that lead them into many adventures. What genre is it? _____

5. Emilio is reading a story about a girl who transports herself into the future through her computer. She discovers a world where people live on Mars and travel with lasers. What genre is it? _____

6. Lauren is reading a story about a proud, selfish pig that won't share its slop with the other pigs. In the end, the pig learns a hard lesson about sharing that everyone can learn from. What genre is it? _____

Now, write one description of a story that fits one of the genres in the box.

_____

_____

_____

What genre is it? _____

DARE TO DIVIDE

Solve each word problem. Write the answer on the line.

1. Mr. Glick paid $121 for tickets to the zoo. There are 11 people in the class. How much was each ticket? <u>$11</u>

2. Kate gives $144 to an animal charity each year. She gives the same amount each month. How much does she give each month? _____

3. Megan has collected 150 marbles. She divided them evenly into 10 bags. How many marbles are in each bag? _____

4. Seashore Community has 240 homes. There are 12 homes in each neighborhood. How many neighborhoods are in Seashore Community? _____

5. Brian counted 70 new puppies at the animal shelter. Each dog had 5 puppies. How many dogs are at the shelter? _____

6. Sam baked 108 cupcakes for the bake sale. She sold them all in 3 hours. If she sold the same number of cupcakes each hour, how many did she sell per hour? _____

Write out each answer from above in word form.

1. ____ ◯ ____ ◯ ____ ____

2. ____ ◯ ____ ____ ◯

3. ◯ ____ ____ ◯ ____ ____ ____

4. ____ ◯ ____ ____ ◯

5. ____ ◯ ____ ____ ____

6. ____ ____ ____ ____ ◯ ____ ____

To solve the riddle, find the circled letters in the secret code. Write the corresponding letters, in order, on the lines below.

E = F	F = D	I = S	N = R
R = M	S = R	V = A	Y = L
X = N	H = E	L = H	U = A
W = L	T = O		

Riddle: What coin doubles in value when half is deducted?

Answer: A ____ ____ ____ ____   ____ ____ ____ ____ ____ ____

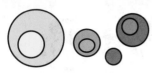

GUIDE WORDS

Do you know how to find words in a dictionary or a thesaurus? They are listed in alphabetical order. Two words appear at the top of each page. They are called **guide words**.

- The first guide word is the first word on the page.
- The second guide word is the last word on the page.

Look at the guide words on each page. Then circle the words that would appear on that page. There could be one, two, or three.

1.

might mirth	shame shear
melon	sheet
milk	shark
mitten	share

2.

brain break	always aunt
brawl	among
breathe	after
brake	author

3.

smoke story	child choice
speaker	choose
storm	chilly
snail	china

4.

present price	wander weather
pretty	wanted
precious	walkway
private	wasteful

5.

endless engine	found function
elephant	foundation
engage	friendly
enemy	fulcrum

6.

refer return	laugh litter
regal	logic
rewind	lively
really	lawful

7.

king known	jeer jester
kingdom	jeep
knoll	jagged
kick	jelly

8.

spoil spring	droop dump
spread	dugout
sprig	dragon
spool	drown

SHAPES AROUND US

Shapes can be moved in different ways. The shape doesn't change, but it looks different.
There are shapes all around us in everything we see.

1. Look at this shape. If you turn it upside down, what will it look like? Draw the shape.

2. Look at this shape. If you turn it once to the left, what will it look like? Draw the shape.

3. What is this shape? _____ Draw an object of the same shape.

4. What is this shape? _____ Draw an object of the same shape.

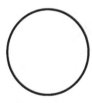

5. What is this shape? _____ Draw an object of the same shape.

6. What is this shape? _____ Draw an object of the same shape.

FACT OR OPINION?

A **fact** is true and can be proven. An **opinion** is how you feel about something.

> **Example:**
> **Fact:** The beach is 12 miles from my house.
> **Opinion:** The beach is too hot today.

Write **F** for **fact** and **O** for **opinion** for each statement below.

1. In the Middle Ages, many people lived in castles for protection. __F__

2. Stone castles replaced wooden ones because they wouldn't burn. _____

3. A stone castle would feel cold during the winter. _____

4. Most people preferred to live in castles rather than in small villages. _____

5. Minstrels and jugglers performed for the king and the queen. _____

6. Banquets and plays were the favorite amusements of the day. _____

7. A castle's outer walls were usually about 12 feet thick. _____

8. Enemy armies camped outside castle walls until people began to starve. _____

9. It was probably frightening to be trapped inside of a castle. _____

10. Prisoners of war were kept in castle basements, called dungeons. _____

Write a fact and an opinion about what it was like to live in the Middle Ages.

Fact: _____

Opinion: _____

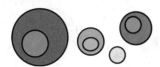

CIRCLE GRAPH

Marco is doing a class survey. He wants to find out his classmates' favorite sweet treats. He put his results in a circle graph.

Answer the questions about the circle graph. Hint: Each section of the circle stands for 4 students.

1. What fraction of students like ice cream?

$\frac{1}{3}$

2. How many students like cookies? _____

3. How many more students like ice cream than fruit? _____

4. What fraction of students like cake? _____

5. What fraction of students like cookies? _____

6. How many students like cookies, cake, and fruit? _____

7. Which two sweets do the same amount of students like? _____

8. How many students were surveyed all together? _____

HURRAY FOR HOLIDAYS!

Proper nouns are words that included the names of countries and people, days of the week, months of the year, and holidays. All proper nouns are capitalized. Use the letter code to fill in each word. Use capital letters correctly.

A B C D E F G H I J K L M N O P Q R S T U V W X Y Z
1 2 3 4 5 6 7 8 9 10 11 12 13 14 15 16 17 18 19 20 21 22 23 24 25 26

People around the world celebrate different holidays. For example, at the beginning of every lunar year, the __C__ __h__ __i__ __n__ __e__ __s__ __e__ celebrate their new year. Each year is represented by

3   8   9   14   5   19   5

a different animal. The year 2006 is the year of the ____ ____ ____.

4   15   7

In the ____ ____ ____ ____ ____ ____, many families around the world celebrate

23   9   14   20   5   18

____ ____ ____ ____ ____ ____ ____ ____ ____. They buy pine trees and stuff

3   8   18   9   19   20   13   1   19

stockings with treats and toys. Winter is also the time when ____ ____ ____ ____ ____ ____

10   5   23   9   19   8

people celebrate ____ ____ ____ ____ ____ ____ ____ ____. This holiday is also known

8   1   14   21   11   11   1   8

as "the festival of ____ ____ ____ ____ ____ ____." Another important holiday takes

12   9   7   8   20   19

place in ____ ____ ____ ____ ____ ____. The people of this country celebrate their 1862

13   5   24   9   3   15

victory over the French army in the Battle of ____ ____ ____ ____ ____ ____. People have

16   21   5   2   12   1

fun by eating traditional Mexican foods and dancing. One of the favorite

____ ____ ____ ____ ____ ____ ____ ____ holidays has always been

1   13   5   18   9   3   1   14

____ ____ ____ ____ ____ ____ ____ ____ ____ ____ ____ ____. On this day,

20   8   1   14   11   19   7   9   22   9   14   7

families gather together to celebrate their good fortune and eat a traditional

____ ____ ____ ____, including a big ____ ____ ____ ____ ____ ____

13   5   1   12   20   21   18   11   5   25

and mashed potatoes. Holidays are special because they allow people from different

____ ____ ____ ____ ____ ____ ____ ____ ____ to honor their history and culture.

3   15   21   14   20   18   9   5   19

What holidays does your family celebrate?

Day 21:
Capitalization

SHAPE CROSSWORD

Read the clues to guess each shape. Write the names of the shapes in the puzzle.

1. p y r a m i d

Across

1. I look like a triangle from the front, but I have 5 surfaces. What shape am I?

3. I have 8 equal sides and 8 equal angles. What shape am I?

6. I have 4 equal sides and 4 equal angles. What shape am I?

8. I am a triangle with 3 equal sides. What kind of triangle am I?

9. I am a polygon with 5 equal sides and 5 equal angles. What shape am I?

Down

2. I am a triangle with one 90° angle. What kind of triangle am I?

4. I look square from the front, but I have 6 surfaces. What shape am I?

5. I am round, but I'm not a circle. You see me in an egg. What shape am I?

6. I am round. You see me in a beach ball or a globe. What shape am I?

7. I am a polygon with 6 equal sides and 6 equal angles. What shape am I?

MEETING THE CHALLENGE

A **personal narrative** is a real-life story about you. It tells about an experience you've had through descriptive details and events. You are the main character!

Think about a time when you were scared or anxious about something. Maybe you were giving a presentation in class or moving to a new neighborhood or school. Think about how you felt and how you met the challenge. Write a personal narrative telling about this event. Provide vivid details to "paint a picture" for the reader. Describe what you felt, saw, and heard.

Title: _____

_____
_____
_____
_____
_____
_____
_____
_____
_____
_____
_____
_____
_____
_____
_____

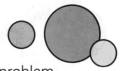

DIVIDE AND CONQUER

Find the two numbers in each chart that can be used to complete the division problem.
Cross out the numbers you don't use. Then write the problem.

1.

9	12	72
36	14	10

_____ ÷ 8 = _____

2.

18	7	24
9	3	28

_____ ÷ _____ = 2

3.

81	84	77
10	8	12

_____ ÷ 7 = _____

4.

10	5	8
7	11	6

56 ÷ _____ = _____

5.

25	12	45
15	5	8

_____ ÷ _____ = 9

6.

70	6	100
60	95	17

_____ ÷ 10 = _____

7.

7	16	21
4	15	9

_____ ÷ 3 = _____

8.

12	6	14
2	8	11

88 ÷ _____ = _____

9.

3	30	6
24	5	32

_____ ÷ _____ = 6

10.

12	144	132
99	10	1

_____ ÷ 11 = _____

11.

7	9	4
6	5	15

54 ÷ _____ = _____

12.

56	96	6
64	9	8

_____ ÷ 8 = _____

PERFECT PUNCTUATION

Read this story. Add the missing punctuation marks.

- Add **quotation marks** around spoken words.
- Add **commas** between words in a series.
- Add a **period** at the end of statements.
- Add a **question mark** at the end of questions.
- Add an **exclamation mark** at the end of sentences that show strong feeling.

Time to get up   Dad called   Maggie and Brett dragged themselves out of the tent   Dad grinned at their sleepy faces

Are you ready for our hike   he asked

Brett groaned   Why do we have to go so early   he whined

Most of the wildlife is out in the morning   Dad explained   I promise you won't be sorry

I'm already sorry   Maggie complained, rubbing the sleep out of her eyes

After eating a good breakfast, they hit the trail with Dad in the lead

A fine gray mist hung over the mountain   Maggie breathed in the smell of wet leaves   pine trees   and wildflowers   Dad was right   Morning on the mountain was beautiful   Brett wasn't so sure   He dragged his feet and kicked rocks along the trail

Would you like to stop up there in that meadow to have a snack   Dad asked

I don't care   Brett grumbled

What a grump   Maggie teased

In the meadow, the hikers sat on a big rock while they snacked on berries   nuts   and raisins

Be very quiet   Dad whispered   We might see something really special

Brett was doubtful   Suddenly Maggie grabbed his arm and pointed to the edge of the forest

A mother deer and her fawn stood silently, watching them   Then the deer slowly walked into the meadow to feed on fresh green grass   Wow, Brett could hardly believe his eyes

After the deer left the meadow, Dad turned to Maggie and Brett

What did you think   Dad asked with a smile

That was amazing   Brett exclaimed   You were right   This was worth getting up for

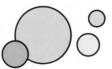 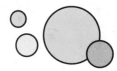

BATTER UP!

Multiply or divide. Then tell if the first product is **less than**, **greater than**, or **equal to** the second product by writing **<**, **>**, or **=** in the baseballs.

1. 9 x 9 10 x 8   **2.** 5 x 5 4 x 7

3. 8 x 7 6 x 11   **4.** 3 x 4 12 x 1

5. 12 x 9 10 x 10   **6.** 4 x 8 7 x 6

7. 6 x 9 11 x 5   **8.** 3 x 8 5 x 4

9. 4 x 4  8 x 2   **10.** 10 x 2 6 x 3

11. 7 x 7 8 x 5   **12.** 3 x 12 6 x 6

13. 6 x 10 12 x 5   **14.** 5 x 9 12 x 4

15. 8 x 8 9 x 7   **16.** 5 x 3 7 x 2

Day 26: Multiply and Divide; Compare

29

VIVID VERBS

Verbs are action words. They tell the action in a sentence.
Verb tense can be **present**, **past**, or **past participle**. Read the examples.

Examples:

Present Tense	Past Tense	Past Participle
bring	brought	brought
speak	spoke	spoken
fall	fell	fallen
throw	threw	thrown

Read each sentence. Then rewrite it using the tense in ( ). The first one is done for you.

1. Maya fell off her bike and scraped her knee. (past participle)

   Maya had fallen off her bike and scraped her knee.
   _____

2. Emma and Sam eat eggs and toast for breakfast. (past tense)

   _____

3. Alonzo rode the bus to school each day. (present tense)

   _____

4. I am using the computer to do my research. (past participle)

   _____

5. The lizard had been running along the fence. (present tense)

   _____

6. Spring flowers bloom outside my bedroom window. (past tense)

   _____

7. The earthquake shook the jars off the shelf onto the floor. (past participle)

   _____

8. Chloe had swum the race with the fastest time. (present tense)

   _____

9. Dad drives us to the mall every Saturday. (past tense)

   _____

10. I chose a great big chocolate sundae for dessert. (past participle)

   _____

SCHOOL DAYS

Use multiplication or division to solve each word problem.
Read each problem carefully to make sure you know what it's asking you to do.
Hint: Solving some problems will depend on the answers from previous problems.

1. Our school has 600 students and 20 classrooms. If there is an equal number of students in each classroom, how many students are in each classroom? __30__

2. Half of the students take buses to school, and 35 students fit on each bus. What is the least number of buses needed to take students to school each day? _____

3. One-third of the students sold cookies in the bake sale. If each student sold $25 worth of cookies, how much money did they make? _____

4. Each class takes two field trips in the fall and two field trips in the spring. How many field trips do all the classes take per year? _____

5. Each teacher needs 12 packs of pencils and 4 packs of notebooks for his or her class. How many packs of each does the school need to order for all the teachers?
_____ packs of pencils   _____ packs of notebooks

6. One-sixth of the students are in the school talent show. If each pair of students is putting on one skit, how many skits will be performed? _____

7. Each student must attend 5 classes per day. How many classes does one class of students attend in one normal school week? _____

8. Mr. Beck coaches 6 soccer teams and 3 tennis teams. Each soccer team has 15 players. Each tennis team has 12 players. How many players does Mr. Beck coach all together? _____

THE MAIN IDEA

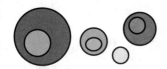 

- The **main idea** tells what a paragraph is mostly about.
- You can usually find the main idea in the **topic sentence**. This sentence tells the most important idea in a paragraph. It usually comes at the beginning or the end of a paragraph.
- **Details** are pieces of information that expand on the main idea. Details help you see a clear picture of the main idea.

Read each paragraph. Circle the topic sentence and underline two supporting details.

1. Poison dart frogs are beautiful but dangerous. They don't bite or sting. Instead, they have poison glands all over their bodies. When a poison dart frog is scared, poison oozes out of its skin. This poison is one of the most toxic in the world.

2. The president of the United States has a very hard job, but at least there are people who help with some duties. These people are called the Cabinet. The president gets to choose members of the Cabinet. Each member looks over a part of the government. Some of these include Homeland Security, Education, and Justice.

3. The upper edge of the Grand Canyon is forested with trees, bushes, and cacti. Every layer of the canyon contains some kind of life. You can see mule deer, coyotes, bighorn sheep, bats, and all kinds of snakes. More than 300 species of birds live there. The Grand Canyon is filled with all forms of life, from the top to the bottom.

4. Saturn is a unique planet because of its system of bright, rings. The rings are so bright, they are fairly easy to see through a telescope. Saturn's rings are made of millions of small particles that orbit the planet together. They are distinct and appear continuous in nature.

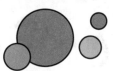
GRAPH IT!

How many astronauts have walked on the moon? Follow the directions below.
The answer will appear in the graph! Hint: The first number in each coordinate is on the x-axis.

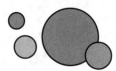

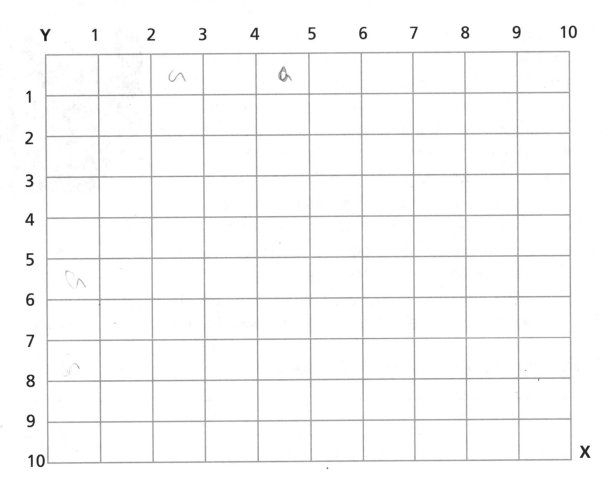

Draw a colored dot on each coordinate:

1. Green (8,3) **2.** Green (6,6) **3.** Blue (3,4) **4.** Green (5,4)
5. Green (5,7) **6.** Green (6,3) **7.** Blue (3,6) **8.** Green (7,5)
9. Green (8,7) **10.** Green (6,7) **11.** Blue (2,4) **12.** Blue (3,5)
13. Green (8,4) **14.** Green (7,7) **15.** Blue (3,3) **16.** Blue (3,7)

Draw a green line to connect the green dots. Draw a blue line
to connect the blue dots.

Answer: _____ astronauts have walked on the moon!

CAUSE AND EFFECT

A **cause** is why something happens. An **effect** is what happens as a result of the cause.
Read the passage. Then answer the questions.

It was 1955 when Rosa Parks climbed onto a bus for a ride home. She was tired from a long day at work. When she took a seat near the front of the bus, she was asked to move. When she didn't, she was arrested. What had she done wrong? Rosa Parks was African American. In 1963, African Americans did not have the same rights as white people. Some of the rules stated that African Americans were not allowed to go to the same schools as whites or drink out of the same water fountains. They also had to sit in the backs of buses. On this day, however, Rosa Parks refused to move. Sick of the injustice, she stayed in her seat. This one act of courage would change the nation forever. Other African Americans started a bus boycott in protest. They stopped taking the buses and walked or used carpools instead. This hurt the bus business and brought the civil rights movement into full force. This one act of courage helped to change the laws of the city as well as the nation.

1. What do you think caused Rosa Parks to stay in her seat?

_____

_____

2. What was the effect of Rosa Parks getting arrested?

_____

_____

3. How did the Montgomery bus boycott affect the bus business?

_____

_____

4. Describe the long-term effect of Rosa Park's brave act. How do you think it affected the city of Montgomery? How do you think it affected the nation?

_____

_____

_____

_____

5. Do you know someone else who did something brave or stood up for a good cause? On another piece of paper, write about this person. Tell what he or she did and why you respect it.

EXACTLY THE SAME

Congruent figures are exactly the same shape and size. Look at each pair of shapes below.
Then write **congruent** or **not congruent**.

1.

not congruent
_____

2.

_____

3.

_____

4.

_____

5.

_____

6.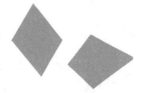

_____

7.

_____

8.

_____

Now, draw a congruent shape to match the shape shown.

9

10.

Read the following poem by Robert Louis Stevenson. Then answer the questions.

My Shadow

I have a little shadow that goes in and out with me,
And what can be the use of him is more than I can see.
He is very, very like me from the heels up to the head;
And I see him jump before me, when I jump into my bed.

The funniest thing about him is the way he likes to grow—
Not at all like proper children, which is always very slow;
For he sometimes shoots up taller like an india-rubber ball,
And he sometimes goes so little that there's none of him at all.

He hasn't got a notion of how children ought to play,
And can only make a fool of me in every sort of way.
He stays so close behind me; he's a coward you can see;
I'd think shame to stick to nursie as that shadow sticks to me!

One morning, very early, before the sun was up,
I rose and found the shining dew on every buttercup;
But my lazy little shadow, like an arrant sleepy-head,
Had stayed at home behind me and was fast asleep in bed.

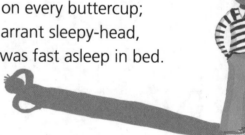

1. What is the rhyming pattern of this poem?
a) aaba aaba   **b)** abcb abcb   **c)** aa bb aa bb

2. What does the boy mean when he says his shadow grows in funny ways?
_____
_____

3. Why does the boy call his shadow a coward?
_____
_____

4. Write two lines from the poem that give the shadow human qualities.
_____
_____

5. Why does the boy call the shadow lazy?
_____
_____

HOW MUCH IS IT?

Look at the coins and the bills in each row. Write the total value of the money.

MONEY	VALUE
1. $1 bill, $1 bill; 25¢ 25¢ 10¢ 5¢ / 25¢ 10¢ 5¢ 5¢	$ 3.10
2. $1 bill, $1 bill; 25¢ 10¢ 10¢ / 10¢ 1¢ 1¢	_____
3. $1 bill, $1 bill, $1 bill; 25¢ 25¢ 5¢ / 25¢ 25¢ 5¢ 5¢	_____
4. $1 bill, $1 bill; 25¢ 25¢ 1¢ 1¢ / 25¢ 10¢ 1¢	_____
5. $1 bill; 25¢ 25¢ 10¢ 10¢ 1¢ 1¢ / 25¢ 10¢ 10¢ 5¢ 1¢ 1¢	_____
6. $1 bill, $1 bill; 10¢ 10¢ 10¢ 5¢ / 10¢ 10¢ 5¢ 5¢	_____
7. $5 bill; 25¢ 25¢ 5¢ / 10¢ 5¢	_____
8. $1 bill, $1 bill, $1 bill; 25¢ 10¢ 10¢ 1¢ / 5¢ 5¢ 1¢ 1¢	_____

9. Add #1 and #3 together. What is the total value? _____

10. Add #2 and #6 together. What is the total value? _____

11. Add #4 and #5 together. What is the total value? _____

12. Add #7 and #8 together. What is the total value? _____

CINQUAINS

A **cinquain** is a five-line poem with a certain number of words or syllables in each line.

Line 1 – The subject (1 word or 2 syllables)
Line 2 – Adjectives (2 words or 4 syllables)
Line 3 – Action verbs (3 words or 6 syllables)
Line 4 – Descriptive phrase (4 to 5 words or 8 syllables)
Line 5 – Synonym or word that sums up the subject (1 word or 2 syllables)

Examples:

Baby	Rain
Soft, cuddly	Fresh, cool,
Cooing, gurgling, smiling	Sprinkling, pouring, pattering
Tiny toes and fingers	Wet on my upturned face
Infant	Shower

Now, write a cinquain of your own. Think of a subject you can describe with vivid adjectives and exciting verbs. Some ideas include: sports, friends, weather, school, animals, and food. Use your imagination!

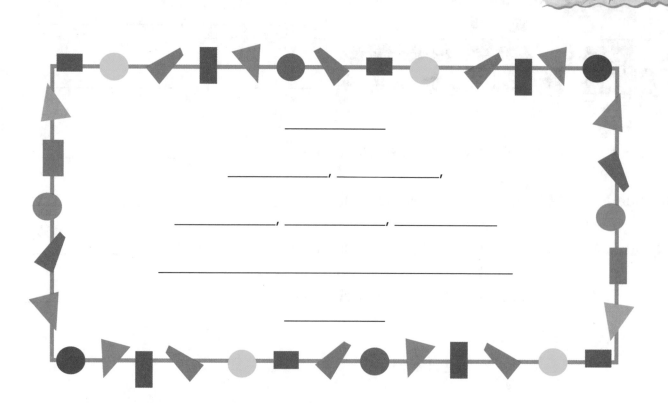

_____

_____, _____,

_____, _____, _____

_____

_____

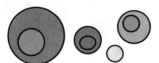

DIVISION SEARCH

There are 18 division problems in this puzzle. Circle each problem.
Hints: Problems can go across or down. A number can be used in more than one problem.

6	25	5	5	12	16	2	8
3	40	9	5	20	8	4	2
24	8	3	1	10	2	30	4
15	5	3	13	2	36	6	6
30	11	7	28	5	60	5	12
14	32	55	7	40	10	4	4
2	9	11	4	18	6	12	3
7	4	5	0	5	21	8	2

CREATIVE COMPARISONS

A **simile** is a comparison using the words **like** or **as**.
Tara's smile was as bright as a ray of sunshine.

A **metaphor** is a direct comparison without using the words **like** or **as**.
The tornado was a monster ripping through the town.

Complete each sentence by writing a simile. Use vivid words for your comparison.

1. Dad's voice boomed like a _____.

2. As fluffy as _____, the clouds floated in the sky.

3. The stars twinkled like _____ on the velvet black night sky.

4. The baby chick felt as soft as _____ against my skin.

5. Nora's hair is as red as _____.

Complete each sentence by writing a metaphor. Use vivid words for your comparisons.

6. Brian Picket was a _____ on the football field.

7. The fans were _____, exploding into cheers when their team scored.

8. Emily is a shy little _____, hiding her face in her mom's skirts.

9. Hunting slyly in the grass, my cat Chester is a _____.

10. The ocean is a _____, holding me in its cool welcoming arms.

Write two similes and metaphors of your own.

11. best friend _____ Compared to: _____

12. new teacher _____ Compared to: _____

13. fast car _____ Compared to: _____

14. fluffy kitten _____ Compared to: _____

STANDARD AND EXPANDED NUMBERS

Numbers can be written in standard or expanded form.

1. 90,925 = <u>90,000 + 0 + 900 + 20 + 5</u>

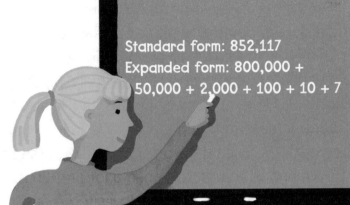

Standard form: 852,117
Expanded form: 800,000 + 50,000 + 2,000 + 100 + 10 + 7

2. 43,602 = _____

3. 794,833 = _____

4. 277,518 = _____

5. 1,355,674 = _____

6. 80,000 + 3,000 + 900 + 70 + 2 = _____

7. 50,000 + 1,000 + 800 + 80 + 5 = _____

8. 600,000 + 60,000 + 2,000 + 0 + 90 + 3 = _____

9. 300,000 + 10,000 + 7,000 + 500 + 40 + 5 = _____

10. 2,000,000 + 700,000 + 20,000 + 5,000 + 500 + 90 + 8 = _____

11. 798,442 =

_____ hundred thousands   _____ ten thousands   _____ thousands

_____ hundreds   _____ tens   _____ ones

12. 6,991,725 =

_____ millions   _____ hundred thousands   _____ ten thousands

_____ thousands   _____ hundreds   _____ tens

_____ ones

THE NEED TO AGREE

Read the following passage about ferrets. Then go back to each sentence.
If the subject and the verb agree, write **yes** on the line. If the subject and the verb do not agree,
rewrite the verb on the line so that it agrees with the subject.

1. Ferrets makes great pets! 2. At the beginning of the year, my fifth grade class adopted a ferret as our class pet. 3. We named him Charlie. 4. Charlie love to play with us all day long. 5. Ms. Gomez told us that ferrets is very smart animals. 6. They learn new tricks very quickly. 7. He jump through hoops. 8. He also beg for food and runs through a maze to find treats. 9. We trained him to use a litter box, just like a cat! 10. Each day, someone in the class take Charlie for a walk. 11. We knows that ferrets need a lot of exercise. 12. He have a special harness and leash. 13. Charlie loves to go outside, but we have to be careful. 14. We don't ever wants him to get loose or lost. 15. When we're in the classroom, Charlie like to chatter at us from his cage. 16. This often gets the whole class laughing. 17. He is also very cuddly. 18. Sometimes he fall asleep right in my arms.

1. _____ make _____   2. _____

3. _____   4. _____

5. _____   6. _____

7. _____   8. _____

9. _____   10. _____

11. _____   12. _____

13. _____   14. _____

15. _____   16. _____

17. _____   18. _____

42

Day 39:
Subject/Verb Agreement

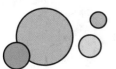

WHAT FRACTION IS IT?

Write the fraction for each set of shaded objects. Then reduce the fraction.

1. 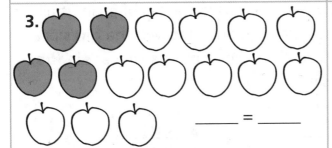 $\frac{8}{10} = \frac{4}{5}$

2. 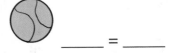 _____ = _____

3. 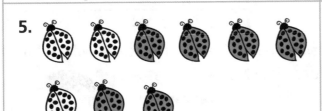 _____ = _____

4. 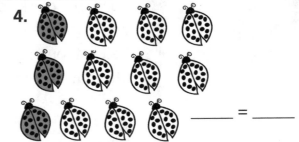 _____ = _____

5. 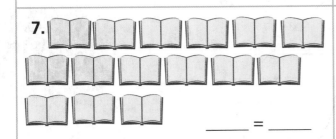 _____ = _____

6.  _____ = _____

7.  _____ = _____

8. 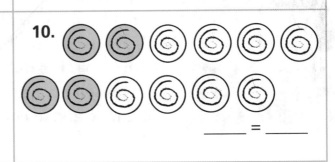 _____ = _____

9. 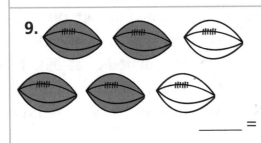 _____ = _____

10. 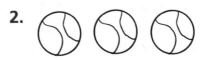 _____ = _____

PICK THE PRONOUN

Write the correct pronoun for each word or words in bold.
Here are some common pronouns and possessive pronouns.

I, me, my, mine	we, us, our, ours	he, him, his
she, her, hers	it, its	they, them, their, theirs

Two elephants escaped the city zoo this morning! As **the elephants** ran down Main Street, people fled in fear. "Why are you afraid of **the elephants**?" a young girl asked. **The girl** came up with a quick solution. **The girl** laid a trail of peanuts all the way back to the zoo. The elephants followed **the girl's** peanut trail without a struggle. Now the elephants are back in **the elephants'** home safe and sound.

1. _____they_____   2. _____   3. _____
4. _____   5. _____   6. _____

Miguel had a fantastic birthday party. **Miguel** invited all his friends from class. **Miguel and his friends** had a great time! First was the arcade. Kim was the best at video games. **Kim** even won a baseball cap. Kim gave **the baseball cap** to Miguel as a gift. Next, the kids ordered some pizza. **The pizza** was delicious, but it left **the kids** wanting more. Next stop, ice cream!

7. _____   8. _____
9. _____   10. _____
11. _____   12. _____

Jing Mae and her family came all the way to the United States from China. **Jing Mae and her family** wanted to join other relatives who had moved years earlier. Jing Mae gave **myself** a doll from China. **The doll** is made from fragile painted glass. Jing Mae and **myself** have become best friends. **Jing Mae and I** share all of **Jing Mae and my** most secret hopes and dreams for the future.

13. _____   14. _____   15. _____
16. _____   17. _____   18. _____

FLYING AMERICA

Look at the United States map below. There are four time zones: Pacific (PT), Mountain (MT), Central (CT), and Eastern (ET):
- Mountain time is 1 hour later than Pacific Time.
- Central time is 2 hours later than Pacific Time.
- Eastern time is 3 hours later than Pacific Time.

> **Example:** If it's 3:00 PM in Seattle, WA, then…
> - It's 4:00 PM in Phoenix, AZ.
> - It's 5:00 PM in St. Paul, MN.
> - It's 6:00 PM in Miami, FL.

Based on the time zone map, answer the questions below.

1. Flight 207 departs San Francisco at 8:15 AM PT.
It lands in New York at 4:15 PM ET. How long is the flight? _____5 hours_____

2. Flight 445 departs Chicago for Miami at 1:30 PM CT. The flight lasts for $3\frac{1}{2}$ hours.
What time should it land in Miami, ET? _____

3. Flight 95 departs Memphis at 3:10 PM CT. It arrives in Dallas at 5:30 PM CT. How long is the flight? _____

4. Flight 604 left Boise at 10:05 AM MT. It arrived in St. Paul 3 hours, 45 minutes later. What time did it arrive in St. Paul, CT? _____

5. Flight 119 departed Seattle, WA, at 9:00 AM. It arrived in Chicago, IL, 4 hours later. After refueling for $\frac{1}{2}$ hour, it departed for Atlanta, GA. It landed $2\frac{1}{2}$ hours later. What time did the flight land in Chicago, CT? _____
What time did the flight land in Atlanta, ET? _____

6. The flight time from Portland to Cleveland is 4 hours, 40 minutes. The flight time from Cleveland to Miami is 3 hours, 10 minutes. Flight 833 left Portland at 11:00 AM PT, stopped in Cleveland for 1 hour, and then flew to Miami. What time did it arrive in Miami, ET?

_____

THE IMPORTANCE OF ORDER

Events in a story must be told in **sequence**, or in the correct order, to make sense.
Read the following passage. Then answer the questions.

Today my grandpa taught me how to make ham and cheese pie. First, you have to gather the ingredients: cheddar cheese, mozzarella cheese, 1 cup of ham cut into chunks, 4 eggs, 2 cups of light cream, salt, pepper, and nutmeg. Then preheat the oven to 375° F. Grease the bottom of a large pie plate. Then scatter the ham to cover the bottom of the plate. Sprinkle the cheese over the ham. Mix together the eggs, cream, salt, pepper, and nutmeg. Pour the mixture over the cheese. Bake the cheese pie for about 40 minutes. Test the pie for doneness by inserting a knife in the middle. If the knife comes out clean, the pie is done. Let the pie cool for at least 10 minutes before serving.

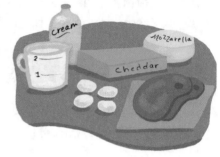

1. What is the first step in making ham and cheese pie?

_____

2. What is the last step in making ham and cheese pie?

_____

3. What do you do right before putting the ham in the pie plate?

_____

4. What do you do right after baking the pie for 40 minutes?

_____

5. Would it matter if these steps were written in a different order? Why or why not?

_____

_____

On the lines below, write steps telling someone how to do or make something. Number your steps in order.

_____

_____

_____

_____

_____

FACTORS OF NUMBERS

A **factor** is a number that divides into another number. Circle the factors for each number.
Write the number of factors you circled in the box.

1. 144
(12, 6, 1,) 9, 10
[3] O

2. 20
10, 4, 5, 2, 1, 20, 15
[ ] S

3. 14
7, 8, 10, 3, 6
[ ] E

4. 36
6, 9, 4, 12, 7, 3
[ ] P

5. 56
16, 12, 10, 9, 5, 18
[ ] A

6. 100
25, 9, 2, 100, 50, 12, 10, 5, 20
[ ] R

7. 18
9, 5, 6, 3, 18, 4, 10
[ ] M

8. 48
8, 10, 4, 15, 5, 9
[ ] I

To solve the riddle, write the letter that goes with each answer on the line.

Riddle: You can keep it only after giving it away to someone else. What is it?

Answer: _____   _____ _____ _____ _____ _____ _____ _____
             0   5   7   3   4   2   6   1

Fill in the missing factors for each number.

9. 16
8, _____, _____, 4, _____

10. 12
_____, _____, 12, 1, _____, 3

11. 28
14, _____, _____, _____, 28, _____

12. 30
_____, 3, _____, _____, _____, 5, 15, _____

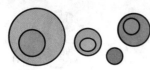 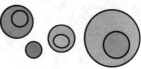

ADVERB ACTION

An **adverb** is a word that tells more about a verb. It tells **how**, **when**, or **where** an action is done.

Example:
How: quickly, silently   **When: today, always**   **Where: outside, there**

Use the clues and the adverbs in the box to complete the crossword puzzle.

Adverbs

fondly	carefully
suddenly	soon
here	quietly
inside	anywhere
early	loudly
weekly	extremely

Across

4. Don't worry; your mom will be here _____.

5. The train left _____, so we were stranded at the station.

7. Our city newspaper is delivered on a _____ basis.

9. Please tiptoe _____ past the sleeping baby's room.

11. Joel is _____ happy about winning the spelling bee.

12. I _____ remember carefree summer days on the beach.

Down

1. The dog _____ jumped up and barked, scaring the child.

2. The kittens are playing _____ the box.

3. We can eat _____ you want, as long as it's not pizza again!

6. Children laughed _____ as the monkeys did tricks.

8. Handle that pot _____, as it is very hot.

10. You can leave your coat right _____ on the bed.

MULTIPLYING WITH DECIMALS

Complete each chart by filling in the answers.

Multiply by	Move the Decimal Point	Example
10	1 place to the right	10 x 5.17 = 51.7
100	2 places to the right	100 x 5.17 = 517
1,000	3 places to the right	1,000 x 5.17 = 5,170

1. Multiply by 10

Input	Output
2.05	**20.5**
0.94	**9.4**
25.42	**254.2**
7.48	**74.8**

2. Multiply by 100

Input	Output
.430	
1.86	
50.09	
.033	

3. Multiply by 1,000

Input	Output
16.3	
.089	
8.51	
0.726	

4. Multiply by 10

Input	Output
3.905	
0.008	
19.4	
90.76	

5. Multiply by 100

Input	Output
0.001	
7.82	
0.292	
84.19	

6. Multiply by 1,000

Input	Output
0.36	
1.39	
100.1	
78.05	

7. Multiply by 10

Input	Output
0.15	
27.18	
8.661	
.907	

8. Multiply by 100

Input	Output
0.355	
7.22	
81.01	
0.909	

9. Multiply by 1,000

Input	Output
545.01	
.180	
.014	
43.00	

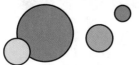
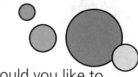

MOVIE MANIA

You have been chosen to review a movie in your local newspaper. What movie would you like to review? You can choose a movie you liked or disliked. Include the following in your review:

- Title of movie
- Main characters
- Summary of plot
- Reasons why you liked or disliked the movie
- Examples supporting your reasons

Example:

Wild Waters was the most interesting movie I've seen all year. The film follows surfing superstar Kelli Thomas on her climb to the world championships in Hawaii. We see Kelli struggle with training and even deal with a devastating injury. The camera work was really exciting! Cameras were strapped to Kelli's surfboard and her arm. The shots were incredible! You felt like you were speeding through the waves along with her. The movie did a great job of showing Kelli's climb from junior competitions all the way to the top. It also showed how hard someone has to work to make it in the surfing world. I would highly recommend this movie to anyone who loves surfing or just wants to take a wild ride through a great story!

4 X 4 MAGIC SQUARES

All rows and columns in these "magic" squares add up to the magic number.
Can you complete the magic squares? Hint: You can only use a number once!

1. All rows and columns add up to 30.

		2	15
3	14		4
	0	7	
	11		1

2. All rows and columns add up to 34.

16		3	9
5	15		
	1		14
2		13	

3. All rows and columns add up to 37.

	6	9	
10		4	
8	1	17	
	12		2

4. All rows and columns add up to 40.

	7		19
5	18	11	
17			12
8		16	

5. All rows and columns add up to 45.

11		5	
	20	12	
19	3		13
			4

Day 48:
Addition

51

SHOWING POSSESSION

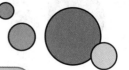

A **possessive** noun shows possession or ownership.
- For a possessive singular noun, add **apostrophe** and **s**. (sled's)
- For a possessive plural noun, add an **apostrophe**. (sleds')
- For a possessive irregular plural noun, add an **apostrophe** and **s**. (men's)

Circle the correct possessive or plural noun to complete the sentence.

1. This _____ bone is buried in the yard.	dogs' **M**	(dog's) **C**	dogs **R**
2. Those _____ toys are in the closet.	childrens' **O**	childrens **L**	children's **H**
3. _____ shoes are on sale this weekend.	Women's **I**	Womens **A**	Womens' **T**
4. Did you hear those _____ giggles?	babies' **C**	babies **W**	babies's **E**
5. Four _____ tails are more than eight inches.	rats **S**	rat's **Y**	rats' **K**
6. The _____ soccer season starts next week.	girl's **U**	girls' **I**	girls **F**
7. We watched _____ playing in the field.	horses **N**	horse's **G**	horses' **P**
8. Are these your _____ backpacks?	students' **A**	student's **D**	students **E**
9. Unpack those _____ contents in the garage.	boxes's **R**	boxes **T**	boxes' **N**
10. My _____ flower garden is in bloom.	grandmas **O**	grandma's **E**	grandmas' **H**
11. Those _____ beds are soft and fuzzy.	puppies **W**	puppies' **G**	puppies's **U**
12. How many _____ will be coming to lunch?	ladies's **S**	ladies' **Y**	ladies **G**

To solve the riddle, write the letters under the nouns you circled in order on the lines.

Riddle: I live in a little house all alone. My house has no doors or windows. If I want to get out, I must break through a wall. What am I?

Answer: A ____ ____ ____ ____ ____   ____ ____   ____ ____ ____ ____

SO MANY CHOICES!

Salad Station has a huge salad bar with many different choices. The choices to go with each salad are tomatoes, olives, cheese, mushrooms, bacon, chicken, onions, egg, broccoli, and sprouts.

How many different combinations can you make? List them below, only once for each combination.

Tomatoes
  olives
  _____
  cheese
  _____
  mushrooms
  _____
  bacon
  _____
  chicken
  _____
  onions
  _____
  egg
  _____
  broccoli
  _____
  sprouts
  _____

Olives
  _____
  _____
  _____
  _____
  _____
  _____
  _____
  _____

Cheese
  _____
  _____
  _____
  _____
  _____
  _____
  _____

Mushrooms
  _____
  _____
  _____
  _____
  _____
  _____

Bacon
  _____
  _____
  _____
  _____
  _____

Chicken
  _____
  _____
  _____
  _____

Onions
  _____
  _____
  _____

Egg
  _____
  _____

Broccoli
  _____

What is the total number of possible combinations? _____

GOOD DESCRIPTIONS

Adjectives describe nouns or pronouns. An adjective tells how many, what kind, or which one. Write three descriptive adjectives for each noun. Use interesting, specific words that tell how something looks, smells, hears, feels, tastes, or acts.

Examples:
Two rabbits.   **Two** **fuzzy** rabbits.   **Two** of **those** **fuzzy** rabbits.

1.
Baby

_____
_____
_____

2.
Ice cream

_____
_____
_____

3.
Rose

_____
_____
_____

4.
Car

_____
_____
_____

5.
Winter

_____
_____
_____

6.
Puppy

_____
_____
_____

7.
Monster

_____
_____
_____

8.
Clouds

_____
_____
_____

9.
Beach

_____
_____
_____

Choose six nouns you described above. Write a sentence using each noun and at least two of your descriptive adjectives.

10. _____

11. _____

12. _____

13. _____

14. _____

15. _____

STEM-AND-LEAF GRAPHS

The **stem** is the first digit of a number. The **leaf** is the second digit of a number. Using **stem-and-leaf graphs** is an easy way to find the range, the mode, the median, and the mean of a group of numbers.

Numbers: 56, 33, 45, 49, 38, 51, 45

Stems	Leaves
3	3 8
4	5 5 9
5	1 6

Range: 56 – 33 = 23
Mode: 45
Median: 45
Mean: 317 ÷ 7 = 45

Find the range, the mode, the median, and the mean for the numbers in each stem-and-leaf-graph. Round to the nearest whole number.

1.

Stems	Leaves
1	3 9
3	5 8 8
4	2 6

Range: _33_
Mode: _38_
Median: _38_
Mean: _33_

2.

Stems	Leaves
7	1 8 9
8	0 4
9	5 7 8 8

Range: _____
Mode: _____
Median: _____
Mean: _____

3.

Stems	Leaves
3	6 6
7	3 4 9
8	2 4 5 7

Range: _____
Mode: _____
Median: _____
Mean: _____

Now, complete each stem-and-leaf graph. Find the range, the mode, the median, and the mean for each group of numbers.

4. 34, 36, 36, 55, 81, 42, 48, 50, 32

Stems	Leaves

Range: _____
Mode: _____
Median: _____
Mean: _____

5. 79, 66, 65, 87, 75, 62, 87, 73, 84

Stems	Leaves

Range: _____
Mode: _____
Median: _____
Mean: _____

6. 25, 29, 18, 25, 15, 19, 27, 22, 20

Stems	Leaves

Range: _____
Mode: _____
Median: _____
Mean: _____

SEARCHING FOR CLUES

When you are reading, you can use context clues to figure out unfamiliar words. **Context clues** are the words around the unfamiliar word that help you understand what you're reading. Read the following passage. Then answer the questions.

Chelsey comes from a daring family. They seem to have no fear and have lived very adventurous lives. Her grandma May flew warplanes in World War II. She has many thrilling stories to tell. Her father, Brent, was a stuntman in the movies. He jumped out of windows, sometimes hurtling ten long stories to the ground. He also rolled and crashed cars. Chelsey's mother owns a skydiving business. So far, her mom has completed 48 jumps. Most of the time her mom jumps in tandem with first-time clients to make sure everything goes smoothly. For beginners, this is much safer than jumping solo. Chelsey is proud of her adventurous family. She is a daredevil in her own right! She has been freestyle skiing for six years. When she sails off the jumps, twisting and turning, she never fails to dazzle the cheering crowd. Chelsey hopes she will make the Olympic team someday.

1. What does the word **daring** mean? How do you know?

_____

_____

2. What does the word **hurtling** mean? What context clues helped you figure out the meaning of the word?

_____

_____

3. Why would jumping **solo** be unsafe for beginning skydivers?

_____

_____

4. What does the word **dazzle** mean? How do you know?

_____

_____

5. Write a sentence using the word **daring**.

_____

6. Write a sentence using the word **dazzle**.

_____

READING BETWEEN THE LINES

The owners of Mimi's Muffins keep track of how many muffins they sell per week.
Using a line graph helps them see how the business is doing. Look at the data in the line graph.
It shows changes over a period of time. Read the graph. Then answer the questions.

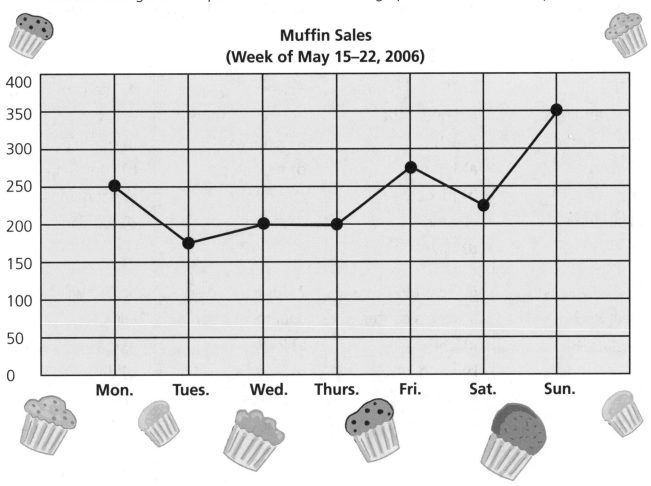

Muffin Sales
(Week of May 15–22, 2006)

1. How many muffins were sold on Tuesday? _____175_____

2. How many muffins were sold on Saturday? _____

3. How many more muffins were sold on Friday than on Monday? _____

4. On which two days were muffin sales the same?_____
and _____

5. Last week, Mimi's Muffins sold 1,600 muffins. Did sales rise or fall this week?
_____

6. How many more muffins were sold on the highest day than on the lowest day?
_____

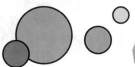

ALIKE AND OPPOSITE

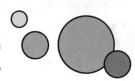

Synonyms are words that mean the same as other words.
Antonyms are words with the opposite meaning as other words.
Look at sentences 1–6 and choose the word that means the same thing as the underlined word.
Then, in sentences 7–12, choose the word that means the opposite of the underlined word.

1. The runner felt weak and <u>tired</u>.
a) exhausted
b) bored
c) amazed
d) surprised

2. The <u>shy</u> mouse hid under the couch.
a) funny
b) friendly
c) timid
d) silly

3. Melissa <u>paused</u> before her speech.
a) wondered
b) hesitated
c) thought
d) stood

4. The carnival ride was <u>frightening</u>.
a) horrible
b) confusing
c) dangerous
d) terrifying

5. "Did you like the book?" Lin <u>questioned</u>.
a) inquired
b) stated
c) demanded
d) suggested

6. He often came across as <u>conceited</u>.
a) evil
b) arrogant
c) noble
d) intelligent

7. Juvia's plane <u>departs</u> at noon.
a) leaves
b) lands
c) arrives
d) goes

8. Dad will <u>repair</u> Eric's car.
a) crash
b) destroy
c) steal
d) fix

9. Tanya hoped the scar was <u>temporary</u>.
a) visible
b) dreadful
c) modest
d) permanent

10. Mario was <u>pleased</u> with his grades.
a) disappointed
b) interested
c) happy
d) insulted

11. Dr. Greer is <u>generous</u> with his patients.
a) giving
b) stingy
c) random
d) disturbing

12. The song will <u>precede</u> the dance.
a) shorten
b) complete
c) pass
d) follow

ROOMS IN THE HOUSE

Perimeter is the sum of the length of all of a shape's sides. To get the perimeter of a room, add all the sides together. **Area** is the amount of space a shape covers. To get the area of a room, multiply the length times the width (l x w). Find the perimeter of each room.

1.

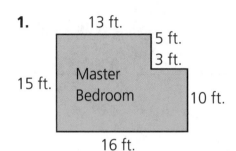

13 ft.
5 ft.
3 ft.
15 ft.
Master Bedroom
10 ft.
16 ft.

Perimeter = ___62 ft.___

2.

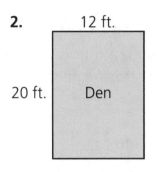

12 ft.
20 ft.
Den

Perimeter = _____

3.

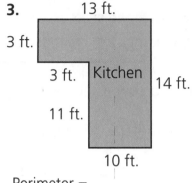

13 ft.
3 ft.
3 ft. Kitchen
14 ft.
11 ft.
10 ft.

Perimeter = _____

Now find the area of the shaded part of each room. Write your answers in square feet (sq. ft.).

4. Bathroom 1

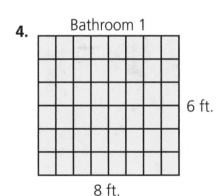

6 ft.
8 ft.

Area = _____

5. Garage

13 ft.
9 ft.

Area = _____

6. Bedroom 1

11 ft.
7 ft.

Area = _____

7. Family Room

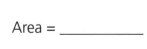

8 ft.
15 ft.

Area = _____

8. What is the total perimeter of all the rooms put together? Perimeter = _____

9. What is the <u>total area</u> of Bathroom 1, Bedroom 1, the Family Room, and the Garage?

Area = _____

NOUNS IN ANALOGIES

Complete these analogies with nouns.
Remember, think of how the words in the first set relate to each other.

> An **analogy** shows a relationship between two words or ideas. For example:
> *Lamb is to ewe as kitten is to _____.*
> To complete the analogy, you need to figure out the relationship of a lamb to a ewe. A ewe is a lamb's mother. So, the missing word should be a kitten's mother, or cat.

1. Milk is to cow as egg is to _____chicken_____.

2. Thermometer is to temperature as ruler is to _____.

3. Mouse is to mice as tooth is to _____.

4. Shark is to fish as snake is to _____.

5. Earth is to planet as sun is to _____.

6. Earthquake is to earth as tidal wave is to _____.

7. Shelf is to shelves as calf is to _____.

8. Claws are to paw as fingernails are to _____.

9. Pacific is to ocean as Mississippi is to _____.

10. Atlas is to maps as dictionary is to _____.

11. Hat is to head as shoe is to _____.

12. Racquet is to tennis as bat is to _____.

13. Rome is to Italy as London is to _____.

14. Boy is to grandpa as girl is to _____.

15. Mexico is to Mexican as Japan is to _____.

16. Coyote is to desert as tiger is to _____.

17. Person is to people as child is to _____.

18. Caterpillar is to butterfly as tadpole is to _____.

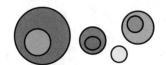

SUMMER CAMP

Aaron, Ellie, Jake, and Nicole love summer camp.
Each child has a favorite activity: canoeing, swimming, hiking, and painting.
Which activity is each child's favorite? Use the clues to find your answer.
Hint: Narrow down your choices by crossing off boxes in the chart.

1. Aaron and Nicole like hiking, but it's not either of their favorite activity.

2. Jake and Ellie's favorite activities are either hiking or swimming.

3. Nicole's best friend thinks painting is the best.

4. Jake's favorite activity used to be swimming.

	Canoeing	Swimming	Hiking	Painting
Aaron				
Ellie				
Jake				
Nicole				

THANK-YOU LETTER

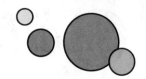

123 Main Street
Littletown, MS 01323
October 17, 2006

Dear Mr. Chase,

    Thank you so much for visiting our class to talk about your work as an astronaut. Your stories were really exciting! The class is now so interested in space travel that we are planning a special field trip to the Air and Space Museum in Washington, DC. You have really inspired us! We appreciate all the time you spent sharing with us and answering our questions. Please visit again soon!

          Sincerely,
          Mrs. Dorian's 5th Grade Class

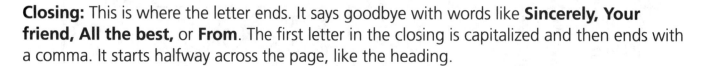

Heading: The heading is your address and the date. Or it can just be the date.

Greeting: This is the opening of the letter. It usually starts with the word **Dear** and ends with a comma.

Body: This is the main part of the letter. Indent each new paragraph.

Closing: This is where the letter ends. It says goodbye with words like **Sincerely, Your friend, All the best,** or **From**. The first letter in the closing is capitalized and then ends with a comma. It starts halfway across the page, like the heading.

Signature: This is where you sign your name.

Think of someone who has done something nice for you. On another sheet of paper, write a thank-you letter to him or her. Explain to this person how much you appreciate what he or she did for you.

Remember to follow these rules:
• Use interesting, specific words.
• Use correct punctuation.
• Use complete sentences.

MAX'S MARKET

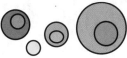

Read the prices on Max's Market sign. Use the information to solve the problems.

Farmer's Market

Peas 13¢ per oz.
Corn 50¢ per cob
Celery 10¢ per oz.
Carrots 12¢ per oz.
Tomatoes 15¢ per oz.
Lettuce $1.15 per head
Red Onions $1.20 per lb.
Sweet Onions $1.45 per lb.
Spinach 75¢ per bunch
Garlic 45¢ per bulb
*16 ounces (oz.) = 1 pound (lb.)

1. Jamie bought $\frac{1}{2}$ pound of peas, 2 pounds of carrots, 4 cobs of corn, and 1 pound of tomatoes. How much did he spend?
_____ $9.28 _____

2. Celery and carrots are on sale for half off today! Ming bought 5 pounds of carrots and 5 pounds of celery. How much did he spend?
_____

3. Carla bought 2 heads of lettuce, 4 bulbs of garlic, 3 bunches of spinach, and 6 cobs of corn. How much did she spend?
_____

4. All green vegetables are on special today. Buy one pound, and get the second pound free! Or, buy one item, and get the second item free! Tyler stocked up on 4 pounds of each green vegetable. He also bought 4 heads of lettuce and 4 bunches of spinach. How much did he spend?
_____

5. Kylie loaded up on onions, tomatoes, and garlic for her special spaghetti sauce. She needs 4 pounds of tomatoes, 6 bulbs of garlic, and 2 pounds of sweet onions. How much did she spend? _____ She paid with a $20 bill. How much change did she receive?
_____

6. Brian needs 1 pound of each vegetable sold per pound or per ounce at Max's Market. How much did he spend? _____
He paid with three $5 bills. How much change did he receive? _____

7. For the holiday, Max reduced the price of each item 5¢. Hanna bought 3 pounds each of red and sweet onions, 3 heads of lettuce, and 3 bunches of spinach. How much did she spend?
_____

8. Corey accidentally knocked over the basket of tomatoes, and 4 of the 15 pounds were ruined! Corey felt bad and decided to buy the rest of the good tomatoes. How much did he spend?
_____

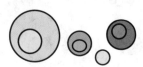 # ABSTRACT NOUNS

Concrete nouns are things you can see, hear, smell, taste, or feel. **Abstract nouns**, on the other hand, are ideas such as knowledge, happiness, and brotherhood. Use the graph to find the abstract nouns below. Each column has a number and each row has a letter. Use the letter and number coordinates to solve the noun puzzles.

Example: 6B = E

	1	2	3	4	5	6	7	8
A	A	K	L	O	R	B	U	X
B	G	D	P	I	V	E	S	N
C	H	T	C	Y	A	W	J	M
D	O	G	E	D	P	H	U	R
E	Y	I	S	W	F	N	K	L
F	E	T	D	M	H	O	Z	C
G	J	A	Q	P	R	I	H	B
H	V	N	F	E	W	S	K	U

1. __f__ __r__ __i__ __e__ __n__ __d__ __s__ __h__ __i__ __p__
   5E 8D 2E 4H 6E 2B 7B 1C 6G 5D

2. ___ ___ ___ ___ ___ ___
   4E 2E 7B 3F 4A 8C

3. ___ ___ ___ ___
   3A 6F 1H 6B

4. ___ ___ ___ ___ ___ ___ ___ ___ ___ ___ ___ ___ ___
   7D 2H 4D 3D 5G 3E 2F 1A 8B 2B 2E 6E 1B

5. ___ ___ ___ ___ ___ ___
   5H 3D 2G 8E 2F 7G

6. ___ ___ ___ ___ ___ ___ ___
   3H 8D 6B 4H 3F 4A 4F

7. ___ ___ ___
   7C 6F 4C

8. ___ ___ ___ ___ ___ ___ ___ ___ ___ ___ ___ ___
   2E 8B 2C 6B 8E 3A 2E 1B 3D 2H 8F 1F

Which of these abstract nouns would you like to have the most? Why?

_____

_____

Use the measurements in the box to solve the problems.
Round to the nearest whole number if needed.

12 inches = 1 foot	3 feet = 1 yard
1,760 yards = 1 mile	1 foot = .30 meter
1 meter = 3.28 feet	100 centimeters = 1 meter
1,000 meters = 1 kilometer	1.6 kilometers = 1 mile
1 kilometer = .62 mile	

1. Brandon runs four 10-mile marathons per year.
How many kilometers does he run per year? ___64 kilometers___
How many yards does he run per year? ___70, 400 yards___

2. Jun needs 8 yards of ribbon to trim the dresses.
How many feet does she need? _____
How many inches does she need? _____

3. The school pool is 20 meters long and 40 meters wide.
How many meters is the perimeter? _____
How many centimeters is the perimeter? _____

4. Justin is 6 feet, 2 inches tall.
How many inches tall is he? _____
About how many meters tall is he? _____

5. Keisha drives 18 kilometers to work each day.
How many meters does she drive round trip? _____
How many miles does she drive round trip? _____

6. Shane measured his bedroom to lay new carpet. His room is 15 feet by 18 feet.
How many meters is the perimeter of the room? _____
How many yards is the perimeter of the room? _____

7. A football field is 100 yards long.
How many meters long is a football field? _____
How many feet long are 3 football fields? _____

8. Mando rode his bike 14 miles along the beach. Karissa rode her bike 20 kilometers
along the beach. Who rode the farthest? _____
How many kilometers did Mando ride? _____
How many miles did Karissa ride? _____

IMPROVE YOUR SENTENCES

Good writing contains specific details and descriptions. To make sentences even better, ask yourself these questions: **Who? What? Where? When? Why? How?**

> **Example:**
> The horse ran.
>
> **What kind?**   **Where?**   **When?**
> beautiful chestnut   across the beach   at sunset
>
> **New Sentence:** The beautiful chestnut horse ran across the beach at sunset.

Now, try your hand at making these sentences better. Remember to think "who," "what," "where," "when," "why," and "how."

1. The soup spilled. _____

2. The giant roared. _____

3. Jen loves flowers. _____

4. The race car crashed. _____

5. Dogs do tricks. _____

6. Mom baked bread. _____

7. Tanner likes to paint. _____

8. The wind blew. _____

9. I like cookies. _____

10. Nate laughed. _____

FOOTBALL FEVER

Touchdown = 6 points
Field goal = 3 points
Safety = 2 points
Extra point = 1 point*

Game = 4 quarters
Football field = 100 yards
First down = 10 yards
Personal foul = 15 yards

*Whenever a team scores a touchdown, it gets a chance to kick an extra point.

Solve these problems about football using the information above.

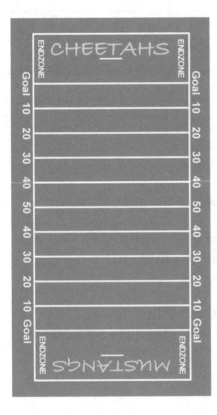

1. The Cheetahs scored 3 touchdowns in the first quarter and 2 in the fourth quarter. They missed two extra points. The Mustangs scored 2 touchdowns in the second quarter, 1 in the third quarter, and 3 field goals in the fourth quarter. They made all their extra points.
Who won the game? ___The Cheetahs___
What was the final score? Cheetahs _____
Mustangs _____

2. Cheetah Jackson Biggs ran from his own 20 yard line to the other team's 42 yard line. How many yards did he gain? _____
How many more yards would he have to gain to get to the Mustangs' end zone and score a touchdown? _____

3. Mustang quarterback Manny Garcia threw the ball from his own 25 yard line. It was caught 50 yards down the field. On what yard line was the ball caught? _____
What percentage of the field did the Mustangs cover?

_____

4. The Mustangs gained 86 yards in the first quarter and 110 yards in the second quarter. They also got called for three personal fouls.
How many total yards did they gain by halftime? _____

5. The Cheetahs are on their own 30 yard line. How many yards do they need to reach the Mustangs' end zone to score a touchdown? _____
How many first downs do they need? _____

6. Mustang Alex Shaw kicked a field goal to win the game by 1 point! The Cheetahs had scored 5 touchdowns, 3 extra points, and 2 field goals. What was the final score?
Cheetahs _____ Mustangs _____

GOOD CONNECTIONS

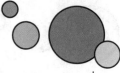

Conjunctions such as **and** and **or** can connect two or more simple subjects to form a compound subject. Compound subjects share the same predicate.

> **Example:** Kittens are soft. Puppies are soft.
> Kittens and puppies are soft.

Use **and** or **or** to write a sentence with a compound subject.

1. Josh is a student in Mr. Chang's class. Maria is a student in Mr. Chang's class.
Josh and Maria are students in Mr. Chang's class.

2. Jaguars live in the rain forest. Toucans live in the rain forest.

_____

3. Tina is a talented dancer. Shiki is a talented dancer. Sonya is a talented dancer.

_____

4. Blue whales are mammals that live in the ocean. Dolphins are mammals that live in the ocean.

_____

5. Shells are on the beach. Starfish are on the beach. Crabs are on the beach.

_____

Conjunctions such as **and**, **but**, and **or** can connect two or more simple predicates to form a compound predicate. Compound predicates share the same subject.

> **Example:** The pizza is cold. The pizza is delicious.
> The pizza is cold but delicious.

Use **and**, **or**, or **but**, to write a sentence with a compound predicate.

6. Cats are fun. Cats are lovable. Cats can be difficult to train.

_____

7. Cell phones are good for safety. Cell phones can be annoying to people around you.

_____

8. Red fire ants should be left alone. Red fire ants should be removed by a professional.

_____

9. Daniel runs very fast. Daniel doesn't like football.

_____

10. Trina lives in the mountains. Trina grows all of her own food.

_____

 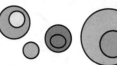

PATTERN PATHS

Look at each set of numbers. What is the pattern? Complete each pattern by writing the missing numbers on the rock, and then write the pattern rule below.

1. 85   75   65   55   45   35   5

Rule: _____ **−10** _____

2.   44   88   704   1,408

Rule: _____

3. 1   4   9   49   81

Rule: _____

4. 24   32   48   72   96

Rule: _____

5. 112   100   88   52   4

Rule: _____

6. 18   33   63   78   123

Rule: _____

7. 40   70   190   250   310

Rule: _____

8. 475   425   275   175

Rule: _____

SURF'S UP!

Read the following passage. Then answer the questions.

Surfers seem to have a language all their own. Some people might think that "surf bum" and "dude" are the only real surf terms, but think again! Surfing has its own special lingo. For example, a "slash" is a rapid turn off a wave that creates a big spray. A "tube" is when the wave is hollow where it is breaking. For some surfers, a tube is the peak experience of surfing. A "stick" is a surfboard, and a "swell" is a wave. A "rip" is a strong current, and a "goofy foot" is surfing with your right foot forward. There are other things you should be aware of as you're riding the waves. In the surfing world, you never want to "drop in." This is when a surfer catches a wave where he or she does not have priority. In other words, there is another surfer already on the wave. You also never want to "wipe out," or fall off your board. Other terms for wiping out are "mullering," "donut," "eating it," and "pounding." So, just do your best to "hang ten" on the "gnarly" waves! You'll be "stoked"!

1. What is considered the peak experience of surfing?

_____

_____

2. Based on the surrounding text, what do you think the word **lingo** means?

_____

_____

3. What should you never do when surfing?

_____

_____

4. What are three other terms for "wiping out"?

_____

_____

5. What is the term for surfing with your right foot forward?

_____

6. Based on the surrounding text, what do you think the word **stoked** means?

_____

DARE WITH DECIMALS

Which number in each group has the largest value? Circle your answer.

1. 0.075
7.50
.0075
(75.00)

2. 5.550
05.50
55.05
5.055

3. 0.024
0.0204
.0024
2.04

4. 9.035
0.935
.0935
0.0095

Which decimal in each group has the smallest value? Circle your answer.

5. 0.30
0.03
0.0003
0.003

6. 0.850
8.005
8.050
0.0085

7. 1.270
.0127
12.170
1.207

8. 0.006
0.060
0.0006
6.00

Write these numbers in order from least to greatest.

9. .058, 0.0058, 5.80, 58.0, 0.580

_____, _____, _____, _____, _____

10. 010, 10.01, 1.001, 100.10, 0.001

_____, _____, _____, _____, _____

11. 9.910, .0910, 0.0091, 9.001, 9.010

_____, _____, _____, _____, _____

12. 537.00, 0.00537, 5.371, 53.07, 0.0537

_____, _____, _____, _____, _____

0.001
0.011
1.00

WRITING STYLES

There are many different styles of writing. Here are a few.
Expository writing gives information and facts. **Narrative** writing tells a story.
Descriptive writing "paints a picture" of a person, a place, or a thing.
Persuasive writing tries to convince someone of something.

Read each prompt below. Then write the style of writing needed—**expository**, **narrative**, **descriptive**, or **persuasive**.

1. _____narrative_____ You went camping on the beach with your family. Tell about your experiences exploring the tide pools and watching the sun set over the ocean. Tell about any special adventures you had.

2. _____ Give instructions on how to fix a flat tire. Write the steps in order so people can follow them easily.

3. _____ Write an article convincing people why it's important to save the rain forests. Support your argument with facts about the negative effects of thousands of acres being destroyed each day.

4. _____ Imagine you are sitting in the middle of a spring meadow. You hear the bees buzzing; you see the grass waving in the breeze. Write details about all the other things you see, hear, smell, taste, and feel.

5. _____ Write an informative article about the pack behavior of wolves in the wild. Explain how packs live and stay together.

6. _____ Do you remember an exciting or memorable birthday? Write about the special events of that day and the gifts you received.

7. _____ Write a letter to your parents giving reasons why you should have a later bedtime. Convince your parents why this would benefit them as well as you.

8. _____ Think about your favorite food. Describe it in detail. Is it spicy or hot? Is it sweet or sugary? Describe how it smells, tastes, and feels in your mouth.

Look at each group of figures. Then answer the question by circling the correct answer.

1. Which figure has a right angle?
a)   b) 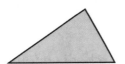   c)

2. Which figure has 6 surfaces?
a)   b)   c)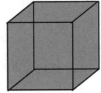

3. Which pair of lines is perpendicular?
a) 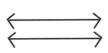   b)   c)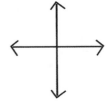

4. Which figure shows an obtuse angle?
a) 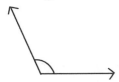   b) 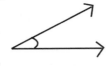   c)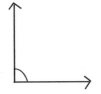

5. Which figure is an equilateral triangle?
a)   b)   c)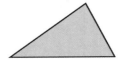

6. Which line shows the radius?
a)   b)   c)

7. Which figure shows an acute angle?
a)   b) 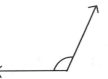   c)

8. Which pair of lines is parallel?
a)   b)   c)

WRITING TO PERSUADE

Persuasive writing tries to convince someone of something. The writer gives the pros or the cons of the subject and tries to get readers to agree with his or her point of view. The writer must use reasons to support his or her opinion.

Choose one of these topics to write about:
- Should students be required to wear school uniforms?
- Should you be able to have any kind of pet you choose?
- Should you be able to watch television whenever you want?
- Should the school allow you to choose the subjects you want to study?

Use this graphic organizer to write your ideas. You can write words, phrases, or sentences.

Topic: _____

First Paragraph

In my opinion:

Three reasons that support my opinion, and examples to support each one.

Paragraph 2

Reason 1	**Examples or details**

Paragraph 3

Reason 2	**Examples or details**

Last Paragraph

My conclusion:

Use your ideas from the graphic organizer to write a persuasive essay.

CALLING ALL COOKS!

Wendy is making chocolate cake for the party. When more people decided to come, she made 5 more cakes. Then even more people decided to come! She made 8 more cakes. Write how much of each ingredient she needed. Hint: Read the measurement equivalents in the box to find your answers.

> 3 tsp. = 1 Tbs.   8 oz. = 1 cup   2 cups = 1 pint
> 2 pints = 1 quart   4 quarts = 1 gallon

Double Chocolate Tower Cake

1 Cake	5 Cakes	8 Cakes
1 cup butter, softened	5 cups	8 cups
1 Tbs. instant coffee		
$1\frac{1}{3}$ cups water		
8 oz. chocolate chips		
5 eggs		
2 tsp. vanilla		
$2\frac{1}{4}$ cups flour		
$1\frac{1}{2}$ Tbs. baking powder		
$\frac{1}{2}$ tsp. salt		
$1\frac{1}{2}$ tsp. cinnamon		

Chocolate Fudge Icing

1 Batch	5 Batches	8 Batches
$\frac{3}{4}$ cup heavy cream		
6 oz. chocolate chips		
$\frac{1}{4}$ tsp. vanilla		
3 cups powdered sugar		
2 Tbs. milk		

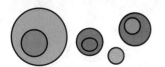 # WRITING TITLES

Rewrite each title using correct capitalization and punctuation.

> **Underline** or **italicize** the titles of books, plays, paintings, magazines, newspapers, television shows, CDs, and movies.
>
> Put **quotation marks** around titles of poems, short stories, book chapters, magazine and newspaper articles, and songs.
>
> **Do Not Capitalize:**
> • Short prepositions (**at**, **by**, **in**, **of**, **for**, **with**, **to**)
> • Short conjunctions (**and**, **but**, **or**)
> • Articles (**a**, **an**, **the**), unless they are the first word in a title

1. tales of a fourth grade nothing (book)
  <u>Tales of a Fourth Grade Nothing</u>

2. mona lisa (painting)
  _____

3. if i had a brontosaurus (poem)
  _____

4. harry potter and the chamber of secrets (movie)
  _____

5. legends of the hidden temple (TV show)
  _____

6. america the beautiful (song)
  _____

7. if i were in charge of the world and other worries (book)
  _____

8. los angeles times (newspaper)
  _____

9. sports illustrated for kids (magazine)
  _____

10. lost in the middle of the night (chapter title)
  _____

11. romeo and juliet (play)
  _____

12. how the tiger got its stripes (short story)
  _____

Write a sentence using each title. Remember to capitalize and punctuate it correctly.

13. ten tricks to teach your dog (magazine article)

_____

14. farmer in the dell (song)

_____

15. julie of the wolves (book)

_____

16. the road to rock and roll (CD)

_____

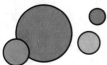
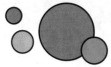

DOG WALKERS

Kevin, Luke, Mira, Tia, and Raul all work as dog walkers to make extra money. Each has a favorite kind of dog. The dogs are dalmations, poodles, beagles, labs, and huskies.

What is each child's favorite dog? Use the clues to find your answer.

Hint: Narrow down your choices by crossing off boxes in the chart.

1. Tham likes beagles less than her favorite, huskies.

2. Raul and Luke do not like labs or beagles.

3. Kevin and the child who likes labs are best friends.

4. Either Luke or Mira likes poodles.

Fill in the names of the children down the side of the chart. Write the names of the dogs across the top of the chart. Now, solve the problem!

GREAT WORDS: THESAURUS

A **thesaurus** is a reference that contains synonyms and antonyms for words. As in a dictionary, words are listed in alphabetical order. Many words have slight differences in meaning. By choosing words carefully, a writer can create a clear picture for the reader. Use a thesaurus to find another word to replace the underlined words in the sentences below. Rewrite the sentence using the new word.

1. "Watch out! That snake could bite you!" <u>said</u> Viet.

_____

2. Jason slipped and <u>fell</u> down the slippery steps.

_____

3. The hikers were <u>hungry</u> when they returned to camp.

_____

4. The mouse <u>ran</u> back to its hole when it saw the cat.

_____

5. Party guests complimented the chef on the <u>good</u> meal.

_____

6. I was too <u>nervous</u> to go to bed after watching the scary movie.

_____

7. Our football team was <u>excited</u> after winning the game.

_____

8. The mountain looked <u>huge</u> against the clear blue sky.

_____

9. <u>Angry</u> fans yelled in protest over the umpire's bad call.

_____

10. I made sure the house was as <u>clean</u> as possible for my guests.

_____

**Day 75:
Using References**

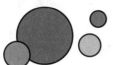

BAR GRAPHS

Read the information in the graph. Then answer the questions.

Favorite Sports Survey

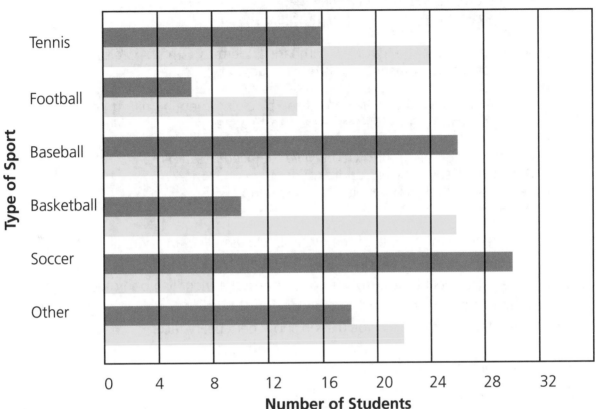

Girls

Boys

1. How many girls like baseball best? _____26 girls_____

2. How many boys like tennis best? _____

3. How many boys and girls like soccer? _____

4. How many more boys like basketball than girls? _____

5. Which sport do boys like best? _____ Girls? _____

6. How many total students were surveyed? _____

USING FIGURATIVE LANGUAGE

Read the paragraph below. Then answer the questions.

> Some words sound like what they mean.
> **crackling fire**   **gurgling creek**
>
> Some words describe things by comparing them to something else.
> **shy as a mouse**   **tall as a mountain**
>
> Some words make things "come alive" by giving them human qualities.
> **dancing rain**   **whispering breeze**
>
> Words can also be used to create vivid, detailed descriptions.
> **Okay:** Small spiders went up the drainpipe.
> **Better:** Tiny spiders scrambled up the drainpipe.

I woke up suddenly in the middle of the night. Darkness filled my room like a thick blanket. I heard the wind moaning outside my window. The trees bent in the wind, holding onto their leaves like protective mothers. As I peeked out my window, not even a friendly moon greeted me. Not one star peeked out from behind the velvet veil of the black sky. Branches screeched and clattered against the side of the house. I hoped morning would soon show her cheery face.

1. Write two comparisons used in the paragraph.

_____

_____

2. What human qualities does the writer give the moon? _____

3. What human qualities does the writer give the morning? _____

4. What words are used to describe the night sky? _____

5. Which two words sound like what they mean? What are they describing?

_____

_____

Write a creative sentence about each of the following topics. Use one example of figurative language described above.

6. pouring rain _____

7. purring kitten _____

8. haunted house _____

9. baking cookies _____

10. car crash _____

FOLLOW THE CLUES

Follow the clues to solve the problems.

Clues

1. Each problem has two steps.

2. Use **( )** as your first step to close off two numbers.

3. Use two operation signs (**x, −, +, ÷**).

4. Use one equals sign (**=**).

Example: 16 _____ 4 _____ 8 _____ 32

Answer: (16 ÷ 4) x 8 = 32

1. 28 _=_ 7 _x_ 8 _−_ 28

2. 77 _____ 13 _____ 3 _____ 38

3. 80 _____ 30 _____ 2 _____ 95

4. 105 _____ 15 _____ 3 _____ 4

5. 6 _____ 12 _____ 9 _____ 18

6. 16 _____ 19 _____ 18 _____ 17

7. 72 _____ 8 _____ 8 _____ 72

8. 57 _____ 25 _____ 15 _____ 480

9. 50 _____ 20 _____ 6 _____ 5

10. 29 _____ 21 _____ 7 _____ 26

11. 98 _____ 49 _____ 25 _____ 50

12. 106 _____ 2 _____ 4 _____ 53

WRITING A PARAGRAPH

A **paragraph** must have a **main idea** and **supporting details**. It should also have a **topic sentence** that tells what the paragraph is about. A good paragraph focuses on the main idea and doesn't stray onto other topics or ideas. Read the following paragraph. Underline the topic sentence. Cross out any sentences that don't belong.

Tigers are known around the world for their beauty, but they face an uncertain future. Rare albino tigers are white. In the last 100 years, tigers faced both natural and human threats. As a result, they are now one of the world's most endangered animals. By the 1970s, tigers that once thrived in certain areas were gone. You can see tigers in most zoos. Today, India is home to about 4,700 tigers. There are only about 7,000 left in the wild. Humans should try to save tigers. These remaining tigers are threatened by many factors. These factors include human crowding, loss of habitat, illegal hunting, and trade in tiger parts used for medicines.

Now write your own paragraph. You can write about anything that interests you, including a favorite relative, a memory, a sport, a food, a pet, or a hobby. Make sure to include:

- a topic sentence
- a main idea
- supporting details

MIXED FRACTION PRACTICE

Add or subtract to solve each problem.

1. Last week, Megan's bean plant was $2\frac{3}{4}$ inches high. This week it grew another $1\frac{5}{6}$ inches. How tall is the bean plant now? _____ **4$\frac{7}{12}$ inches** _____

2. Jordan ate $\frac{1}{3}$ of the pizza yesterday. His brother ate $\frac{1}{4}$ of the pizza today. If their dad ate another $\frac{1}{4}$, how much of the pizza is left? _____

3. Isel has $\frac{1}{5}$ left from one bottle of glue and $\frac{2}{3}$ left from another bottle. If she poured all the glue into one bottle, how much would she have? _____

4. Kenny sold $\frac{3}{4}$ of his tickets for the raffle. Yasmin sold $\frac{7}{12}$ of her tickets. Barry sold $\frac{4}{6}$ of his tickets. Each child started with 12 tickets. How many tickets did they sell all together? _____
_____

5. Tammy cut the cake into 20 pieces. Skip ate $\frac{1}{10}$ of the cake. Kristin ate $\frac{2}{5}$ of the cake. Caleb ate $\frac{1}{5}$ of the cake. How many pieces of cake are left over? _____

6. Riley uses $\frac{1}{6}$ tank of gas to drive to work. If he starts with $\frac{8}{12}$ of a tank, how much does he have left when he gets to work? _____

7. $3\frac{1}{3} + 8\frac{9}{12} =$

8. $5\frac{4}{6} - 2\frac{1}{4} =$

9. $7\frac{3}{8} - 6\frac{3}{4} =$

10. $4\frac{1}{8} + 4\frac{3}{16} =$

11. $14\frac{3}{9} - 10\frac{2}{6} =$

12. $3\frac{9}{10} + 7\frac{3}{5} =$

MARVELOUS MYTHS

Myths are make-believe stories that explain how things came to be. They usually tell about things that happen in nature. Myths are usually passed down from generation to generation. Read the myth below.

How the Tiger Got Its Stripes

Long ago, tigers used to be bright orange all over. They shone almost as bright as the sun. Then one summer, the sun scorched the earth. Plants shriveled in the heat, and rivers dried up. All the animals of the jungle were looking for shade. The tigers found a perfect place to hide under the cool, spiny leaves of the palm trees. As they rested and played, they didn't realize that the sun burned right through those thin, spiny leaves, leaving black strips on the beautiful orange fur. And that is why the tiger has stripes.

Choose one of these topics to write a myth of your own. Or, use your own idea.

Why penguins can't fly	How the giraffe got its long neck
How the camel got its hump	Why the moon changes
Why the sun sets	Why the seasons change
Why snakes don't have legs	Why dinosaurs are extinct

Title of Myth:

Long ago, _____

_____

_____

_____

_____

_____

_____

_____

_____

_____

And that is why _____

TAKE A GUESS

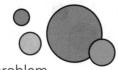

Probability is a way to guess, or estimate, an answer to a problem.
It can help you come close to an answer without actually solving a problem.

> **Example:** There are 5 marbles in the bag: green, blue, yellow, red, and purple.
> If you reach into the bag, how likely is it you will get a red marble?
>
> **Answer:** 1 in 5 or $\dfrac{1}{5}$

1. How likely is it that the spinner will land on orange? Answer: $\dfrac{1}{8}$

2. How likely is it that the spinner will land on blue? Answer: _____

3. How likely is it that the spinner will land on purple or yellow?
Answer: _____

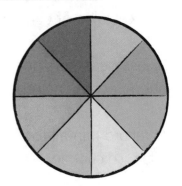

In this jar of candies…
- 10 are cherry.
- 5 are lemon.
- 10 are lime.
- 3 are grape.
- 2 are orange.

4. How likely is it that you will grab a grape candy? Answer: _____

5. How likely is it that you will grab a cherry or a lime candy? Answer: _____

6. How likely is it that you will grab a lemon or an orange candy? Answer: _____

7. How likely is it that you will roll an E? Answer: _____

8. How likely is it that you will roll an A, a C, or an F?
Answer: _____

9. How likely is it that you will roll a C or a D in three rolls?
Answer: _____

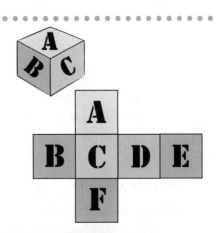

WHERE DO I FIND IT?

Circle the reference where you would look to find the following information.

1. the building of the Statue of Liberty
(encyclopedia)   dictionary   glossary   atlas

2. definitions for words found in the third chapter of a science book
index   table of contents   glossary   almanac

3. last weekend's hockey scores
phone book   newspaper   atlas   dictionary

4. record rainfall totals from 1988
atlas   dictionary   encyclopedia   almanac

5. pages relating to tornadoes
glossary   index   newspaper   phone book

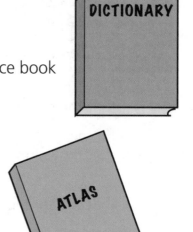

6. rain forests of South America
dictionary   table of contents   encyclopedia   newspaper

7. this week's weather forecast
newspaper   encyclopedia   dictionary   atlas

8. chapter about black widow spiders
glossary   table of contents   index   encyclopedia

9. pages relating to the food pyramid
dictionary   glossary   almanac   index

10. area codes for your county
encyclopedia   index   phone book   table of contents

11. all homerun records set in baseball
atlas   newspaper   almanac   dictionary

12. how many miles it is from your town to the capital city
almanac   encyclopedia   index   atlas

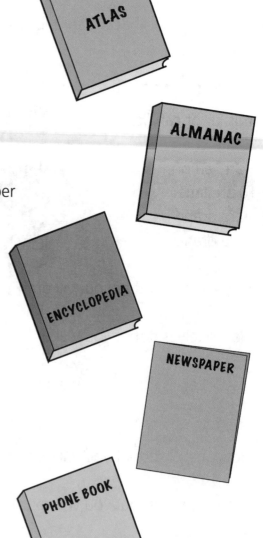

PERFECTING PERCENTAGES

Solve each problem. Some answers may have decimals.

1. 45% of 100 = ___45___   **2.** 15% of 25 = _____   **3.** 50% of 200 = _____

4. 22% of 120 = _____   **5.** 60% of 35 = _____   **6.** 75% of 300 = _____

7. 10% of 168 = _____   **8.** 85% of 536 = _____   **9.** 64% of 80 = _____

Solve each word problem.

10. Flowers are 25% off at Plant Depot. Tad bought 4 plants for $1.25 each. How much money did he save? _____

11. Price One is having a blowout sale. All merchandise is 40% off! Kang bought 3 T-shirts for $5.00 each and a pair of shoes for $12.50.
How much money did she spend? _____

12. Zane's grades are in the top 10% of his class. There are 40 students in all. How many students are in the top 10%? _____

13. Kelli threw 60% of the pitches in last night's softball game. All together, 160 pitches were thrown. How many pitches did Kelli throw? _____

14. Leather jackets are on sale for 30% off. Each jacket costs $96.00. How much did Lisa spend on two jackets? _____

15. Tyra's hourly rate at work has increased 15% per year since she started two years ago. She started at $5.50 per hour. Hint: Figure her last increase based on the previous year's salary. How much is Tyra making per hour now? _____

GRAPHIC ORGANIZERS

A **graphic organizer** is used for organizing information. It is a diagram in which you can list key words, phrases, and ideas before you begin writing. It helps you to organize your main idea and supporting details. Use the main ideas and the supporting details below to complete this graphic organizer.

Main Ideas and Supporting Details

Size of small cat   Baby called "puggle"   Lives in burrows near fresh water
Young   From Australia   Webbed feet
Bill like a duck   Eats worms and snails   Flat tail like a beaver
Furry   Hatches from eggs   Daily life
Loves to swim   Drinks milk from mother   Born without hair

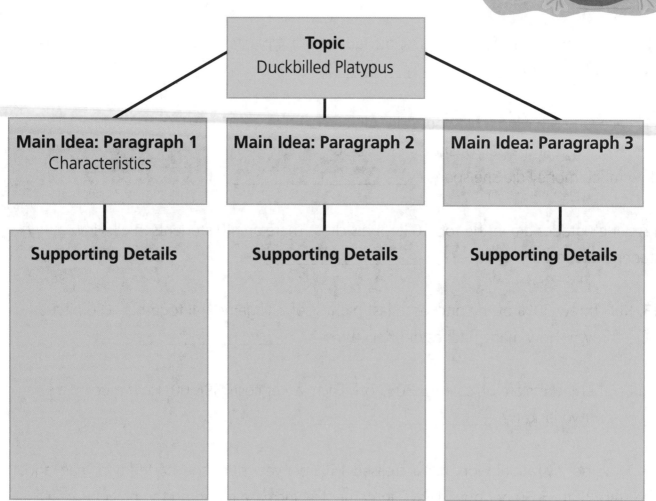

Topic
Duckbilled Platypus

Main Idea: Paragraph 1
Characteristics

Main Idea: Paragraph 2

Main Idea: Paragraph 3

Supporting Details

Supporting Details

Supporting Details

Now, think of a topic you would like to research. Use encyclopedias, the Internet, and other resources to find information about the topic. Then arrange the information in a graphic organizer.

THREE CHEERS FOR BASEBALL!

Use the information on the scoreboard to solve the problems.

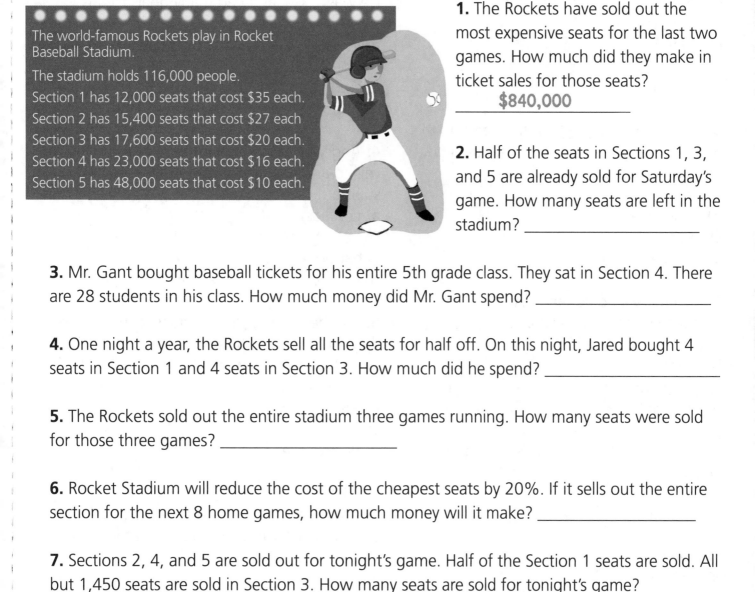

The world-famous Rockets play in Rocket Baseball Stadium.

The stadium holds 116,000 people.

Section 1 has 12,000 seats that cost $35 each.

Section 2 has 15,400 seats that cost $27 each

Section 3 has 17,600 seats that cost $20 each.

Section 4 has 23,000 seats that cost $16 each.

Section 5 has 48,000 seats that cost $10 each.

1. The Rockets have sold out the most expensive seats for the last two games. How much did they make in ticket sales for those seats?
$840,000

2. Half of the seats in Sections 1, 3, and 5 are already sold for Saturday's game. How many seats are left in the stadium? _____

3. Mr. Gant bought baseball tickets for his entire 5th grade class. They sat in Section 4. There are 28 students in his class. How much money did Mr. Gant spend? _____

4. One night a year, the Rockets sell all the seats for half off. On this night, Jared bought 4 seats in Section 1 and 4 seats in Section 3. How much did he spend? _____

5. The Rockets sold out the entire stadium three games running. How many seats were sold for those three games? _____

6. Rocket Stadium will reduce the cost of the cheapest seats by 20%. If it sells out the entire section for the next 8 home games, how much money will it make? _____

7. Sections 2, 4, and 5 are sold out for tonight's game. Half of the Section 1 seats are sold. All but 1,450 seats are sold in Section 3. How many seats are sold for tonight's game?

_____

8. Each season, Kidz Toys buys 25 seats in each section for its employees. How much money does Kidz Toys spend for these seats? _____

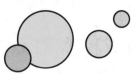
WORDS IN CONTEXT
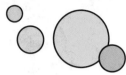

Read the sentences carefully. Which word fits best in the blank?
Use context clues in the sentences to help you choose the correct word.

1. Tonti grabbed a sandwich from fridge. She hadn't eaten since breakfast and was _____.
a) nauseated
b) ravenous
c) amazed
d) irritated

2. Michael was always at the top of his class. He was _____ and had many goals for his future.
a) impossible
b) unrealistic
c) ambitious
d) puzzling

3. Sofia loved the _____ of the beach in the morning. Only the sounds of seagulls and foaming waves washed over her.
a) clamor
b) arrogance
c) serenity
d) turbulence

4. Angry protestors filled the streets. The yelling and shouting increased as the _____ spun out of control.
a) conflict
b) courage
c) harmony
d) disaster

5. Kristin is very quiet and shy. Unlike her outgoing brother, she is quite _____.
a) introverted
b) friendly
c) intelligent
d) disgraceful

6. First he chewed up my shoes, and then he dug up the flower garden. As _____ as he is, we still love our new puppy.
a) determined
b) fascinating
c) considerate
d) destructive

7. I can _____ the cold winds and snow. I just don't know if I can deal with the hot summers.
a) remember
b) tolerate
c) surrender
d) suffocate

8. Your speech should _____ people to recycle to help save the environment. Tell them how easy it is just to save water or recycle newspapers.
a) precaution
b) confuse
c) restrain
d) influence

9. Each painting has its own _____ style. The colors and the subjects are quite unique.
a) distinct
b) desperate
c) foreign
d) terrific

10. A butterfly's life cycle is one of change. During the pupa stage a caterpillar will _____ into a beautiful butterfly.
a) survive
b) resume
c) launch
d) transform

Day 87:
Context Clues

 # USING VARIABLES

A **variable** is a letter that represents an unknown number in an equation. To solve a problem with a variable, use one of the four math operations (addition, subtraction, multiplication, division). Use variables to solve these problems.

Example: $12n = 36$

To solve, divide both sides by 12. $\dfrac{12n}{12} = \dfrac{36}{12}$

Answer: $n = 3$

---

1. An unknown number multiplied by 7 equals 77. What is the number?

$7n = 77$

2. An unknown number multiplied by 9 equals 54. What is the number?

$9n = 54$

3. Brit divided her markers into 10 groups of 4. How many markers did she start with? Write and solve the problem.

4. Darryl has 8 groups of an unknown number that equals 32. What number is in each group? Write and solve the problem.

5. Lily divided her cupcakes into 5 groups of 3. How many cupcakes did she start with? Write and solve the problem.

6. An unknown number of ladybugs plus 48 equals 66. What number of ladybugs is it? Write and solve the problem.

THE BENEFITS OF TRAVEL

Drawing a conclusion is forming a thought based on what you already know of the facts and the details in the text. These facts and details should lead you to a logical conclusion. Read the passage below. Then answer the questions.

Traveling is a lot of fun, but it can also be educational. Traveling to different places and meeting new people can teach you a lot about the world. You might see different environments, like deserts, mountains, jungles, or big cities. Each place might be home to different kinds of animals. In Africa you can see elephants and lions. In Australia you can see koalas and kangaroos. In the mountains of North America you can see bear and deer. Visiting new places can also teach you about the people who live there. You might experience different languages, foods, traditions, and clothing. You can visit museums to learn about a place's history and art. Travel is not only an adventure; it is also a learning experience. You will learn to appreciate a whole new world you never knew before!

1. Draw a conclusion about the purpose of this passage.

_____

_____

2. What details support this conclusion?

_____

_____

3. Describe what you think you might learn on a visit to Japan.

_____

_____

4. What details made you draw this conclusion?

_____

_____

5. What do you think would happen if people never traveled?

_____

_____

6. Think of a place in the world you would like to visit. What do you think you might learn during your stay? Write about it below.

_____

_____

_____

_____

MYSTERY MATH SQUARES

Follow these rules to fill in the missing numbers and solve the math squares.

1. Use the numbers 1 through 9 to complete the equations.
2. Use each number only once.
3. Each row is a math equation. Each column is a math equation.
4. Do multiplication and division before addition and subtraction.

1.

	+		−		4
+		−		+	
	+		+		16
+		−		X	
	−		−		−3

| 19 | −12 | 17 |

2.

	+		X		23
X		X		X	
	−		+		8
+		+		+	
	−		−		−11

| 39 | 10 | 41 |

3.

	+		÷		9
X		−		+	
	−		−		−11
−		−		−	
	X		−		−3

| 9 | −4 | −1 |

4.

	X		−		4
−		+		X	
	−		−		−9
X		÷		+	
	÷		−		1

| −23 | 4 | 38 |

ANSWER KEY

Page 4
Underline: Out, Down, Around, Onto, Into, Off, Over, Into
Poems will vary.

Page 5
2. 8,660; circle the second-from-the-right 6
3. 17,400; circle 4
4. 93,000; circle 3
5. 212,000; circle 2
6. 110,000; circle the second-from-the-left 1
7. 25,540; circle 4
8. 860,000; circle 6
9. 66,800; circle 8
10. 19,000; circle 9
11. 500,200; circle 2
12. 680,000; circle 8
13. 35,740; circle 4
14. 71,000; circle 1
Answer: A yard sale

Page 6
neat street
fake lake
blue shoe
smitten kitten
glad dad
hot spot
big pig
lazy daisy
hairy berry
rude mood
wet pet
small ball
cool ghoul
legal eagle

Page 7

Value						
$3.52	0	3	2	0	0	2
$6.23	1	1	0	2	0	3
$4.78	0	4	3	0	0	3
$3.92	1	3	3	1	1	2
$7.03	1	2	0	0	0	3
$5.16	1	0	0	1	1	1
$9.44	4	1	1	4	0	4
$2.65	0	2	2	1	1	0
$8.90	1	2	3	1	1	0
$4.86	0	4	3	1	0	1
$3.99	0	3	2	2	0	4
$9.67	1	2	1	1	1	2

1. $2.73
2 $1 bills, 2 quarters, 2 dimes, 3 pennies
2. $2.15
2 $1 bills, 1 dime, 1 nickel

Page 8
2. babies   3. wolves
4. boxes   5. men
6. flies   7. mice
8. bands   9. elves
10. watches   11. monkeys
12. cars   13. glasses
14. sheep   15. children

Page 9

1.
11	2	1
3	7	4
0	5	9

2.
10	2	4
1	6	9
3	8	3

3.
10	6	4
8	9	3
2	5	13

4.
14	7	2
6	12	5
3	4	16

5.
12	13	7
17	10	5
3	9	20

6.
10	15	20
13	14	18
22	16	7

Page 10
2. there; they're; their
3. fowl; foul
4. flour; flower
5. marry; merry
6. its; it's
7. so; sew; sow
8. whether; weather
9. wood; would
10. to; too; two
11. do; dew; due
12. heel; heal; he'll

Page 11
2. $14\frac{2}{3}$ 3. $9\frac{1}{5}$
4. $17\frac{8}{9}$ 5. $4\frac{1}{4}$
6. 6   7. $9\frac{3}{10}$
8. $5\frac{1}{5}$ 9. $18\frac{1}{3}$
10. $8\frac{1}{2}$ 11. >
12. >   13. <
14. =   15. =
16. >

Page 12

ADJ N   A ADJ N   V
1. Wild Willy watched the wavy worms wiggle and wobble.
ADJ   N   V   A ADJ ADJ N
2. Pretty Patty picked a pricey pink dress.
N   V   A N P V P N
3. Oliver opened the oven to check on oily omelets.
ADJ   N   V   ADJ   N   P V
4. Cheery Charlie chose chunky cheese to chew.
N   A   N   V   N PADJ ADJ N
5. Harry the hippo helped Hanna hide huge holey hats.
ADJ   N   V   ADJ   N   P AN
6. Funny Frannie found flat flowers under the floor.
ADJ   N   V   N   P ADJ ADJ N
7. Bored Benny bought bundles of bright blue balloons.
N   V   N PADJ ADJ N
8. Jessica Jones juggled jars of juicy jiggling jelly.
ADJ N   V   P A N
9. Crazy cats crooned and cried under the moon.
ADJ   N   V   ADJ N P   ADJ N
10. Dizzy Darryl drove his dusty dog in his dirty truck.
ADJ   ADJ   N   V   N
11. Lumpy, lounging lions laughed and licked lollipops.
A N PADJ N   V   ADJ ADJ N   P A N
12. A team of tired tigers tasted ten tangy tacos for a treat.

Page 13
2. early   3. early
4. late   5. late
6. early   7. early
8. late   9. early
10. early

Page 14
2. about 80 feet long and weighs about 12 tons
3. with whistles
4. Yes; Because it's louder than a jet engine and a jet engine is louder than a lion.

5. A baleen whale is a whale that eats by filtering tiny plankton and fish from the water.
6. It gulps mouthfuls of plankton and fish, while its throat expands to form a large pouch. The water is forced through baleen plates hanging from the upper jaw, which catches the food.

Page 15
Row 1: 4, 81, 144, 16, 36, 100
Row 2: 121, 25, 1, 9, 64, 49
Circle the following numbers:
Troy: 144, 4, 9, 81, 49, 1, 100
Tanya: 16, 25, 36, 121, 64
Troy counted the most stars.

Page 16
Sentences will vary.

Page 17
2. 90.7   3. 26.9
4. 65.94   5. 84.03
6. 40.85   7. 97.15
8. 48.04   9. 23.03
10. 31.83   11. 11.84
12. 20.93   13. 74.44
14. 3.84   15. 70.91
16. 21.7

Page 18
2. myth
3. fairy tale
4. mystery
5. science fiction
6. fable
Story descriptions will vary.

Page 19
2. $12   3. 15
4. 20   5. 14
6. 36
Answer: A half dollar

Page 20
1. milk; shark, share
2. brawl, brake; among
3. speaker, storm, snail; chilly, china
4. pretty; wanted, wasteful
5. engage, enemy; foundation, friendly, fulcrum
6. regal; lawful
7. kingdom, knoll; jelly
8. spread, sprig, spool; dugout, drown

Page 21
1.   2.
3. cube; drawings will vary
4. sphere; drawings will vary
5. octagon; drawings will vary
6. cylinder; drawings will vary

Page 22
2. F   3. O
4. O   5. F
6. O   7. F
8. F   9. O
10. F
Facts and opinions will vary.

Page 23
2. 12 students
3. 12 students
4. $\frac{2}{12}$ or $\frac{1}{6}$
5. $\frac{3}{12}$ or $\frac{1}{4}$
6. 24 students
7. candy and cake
8. 48 students

Page 24
dog
winter
Christmas
Jewish
Hanukkah
lights
Mexico
Puebla
American
Thanksgiving
meal
turkey
countries

Page 25
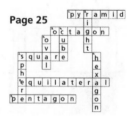

Page 26
Narratives will vary.

Page 27
1. $72 \div 8 = 9$
2. $18 \div 9 = 2$
3. $84 \div 7 = 12$
4. $56 \div 8 = 7$
5. $45 \div 5 = 9$
6. $60 \div 10 = 6$
7. $21 \div 3 = 7$
8. $88 \div 11 = 8$
9. $30 \div 5 = 6$
10. $132 \div 11 = 12$
11. $54 \div 9 = 6$
12. $64 \div 8 = 8$

Page 28

"Time to get up!" Dad called. Maggie and Brett dragged themselves out of the
Dad grinned at their sleepy faces.
"Are you ready for our hike?" he asked.
Brett groaned. "Why do we have to go so early?" he whined.
"Most of the wildlife is out in the morning," Dad explained.
"I promise you won't be sorry."
"I'm already sorry," Maggie complained, rubbing the sleep out of her eyes.
After eating a good breakfast, they hit the trail with Dad in the lead.
A fine gray mist hung over the mountain. Maggie breathed in the smell of wet pine trees and wildflowers. Dad was right. Morning on the mountain was beautiful.
Brett wasn't so sure. He dragged his feet and kicked rocks along the trail.
"Would you like to stop up there in that meadow to have a snack?" Dad asked.
"I don't care," Brett grumbled.
"What a grump," Maggie teased
In the meadow, the hikers sat on a big rock while they snacked on berries, nuts, and raisins.
"Be very quiet," Dad whispered. "We might see something really special."
Brett was doubtful. Suddenly Maggie grabbed his arm and pointed to the edge of the forest. A mother deer and her fawn stood silently, watching them. Then the deer slowly walked into the meadow to feed on fresh green grass. Wow, Brett could hardly believe his eyes! After the deer left the meadow, Dad turned to Maggie and Brett.
"What did you think?" Dad asked with a smile. "That was amazing!" Brett exclaimed. "You were right. This was worth getting up for."

Page 29
1. >   2. <   3. <
4. =   5. >   6. <
7. <   8. >   9. =
10. >   11. >   12. =
13. =   14. <   15. >
16. >

Page 30
2. Emma and Sam ate eggs and toast for breakfast.
3. Alonzo rides the bus to school each day.
4. I had used the computer to do my research.
5. The lizard runs along the fence.
6. Spring flowers bloomed outside my bedroom window.
7. The earthquake had shaken the jars off the shelf onto the floor.
8. Chloe swims the race with the fastest time.
9. Dad drove us to the mall every Saturday.
10. I had chosen a great big chocolate sundae for dessert.

Page 31
2. 9 buses
3. $5,000
4. 80 field trips
5. 240 packs of pencils; 80 packs of notebooks
6. 50 skits
7. 750 classes
8. 126 players

Page 32

Page 33

Answer: 12 astronauts have walked on the moon!

Page 34

1. She was sick of the injustice of African Americans having to sit in the backs of buses.
2. African Americans in Montgomery started a bus boycott in protest.
3. It hurt the bus business because African Americans weren't riding the buses anymore.
4. The Montgomery bus boycott brought attention to the civil rights movement. It showed the nation how unfair these laws were for African Americans and eventually helped change the laws.
5. Answers will vary.

Page 35

2. congruent
3. not congruent
4. congruent
5. not congruent
6. congruent
7. congruent
8. not congruent
9.–10. Shapes drawn should be congruent.

Page 36

1. c
2. It doesn't grow like a regular child; it shoots up tall or gets tiny depending on where the sun is in the sky.
3. Because he sticks close to the boy.
4. Any two: He hasn't got a notion of how children ought to play,
And he can only make a fool of me in every sort of way.
But my lazy little shadow, like an arrant sleepy-head, Had stayed at home behind

me and was fast asleep in bed.
5. Because he didn't get up with the boy and stayed in bed sleeping.

Page 37

2. $4.57   3. $4.15
4. $4.88   5. $2.24
6. $3.65   7. $5.70
8. $4.58   9. $7.25
10. $8.22   11. $7.12
12. $10.28

Page 38

Cinquains will vary.

Page 39

Page 40

Similes and metaphors will vary.

Page 41

2. 40,000 + 3,000 + 600 + 0 + 2
3. 700,000 + 90,000 + 4,000 + 800 + 30 + 3
4. 200,000 + 70,000 + 7,000 + 500 + 10 + 8
5. 1,000,000 + 300,000 + 50,000 + 5,000 + 600 + 70 + 4
6. 83,972
7. 51,885
8. 662,093
9. 317,545
10. 2,725,598
11. 7 hundred thousands, 9 ten thousands, 8 thousands, 4 hundreds, 4 tens, 2 ones
12. 6 millions, 9 hundred thousands, 9 ten thousands, 1 thousand, 7 hundreds, 2 tens, 5 ones

Page 42

1. make   2. yes
3. yes   4. loves
5. are   6. yes
7. jumps   8. begs
9. yes   10. takes
11. know   12. has
13. yes   14. want
15. likes   16. yes
17. yes   18. falls

Page 43

2. $\frac{3}{6} = \frac{1}{2}$ 3. $\frac{4}{16} = \frac{1}{4}$
4. $\frac{3}{12} = \frac{1}{4}$ 5. $\frac{4}{6} = \frac{2}{3}$
6. $\frac{4}{8} = \frac{1}{2}$ 7. $\frac{15}{15} = 1$
8. $\frac{2}{10} = \frac{1}{5}$ 9. $\frac{4}{6} = \frac{2}{3}$
10. $\frac{4}{12} = \frac{1}{3}$

Page 44

2. them   3. She
4. She   5. her
6. their   7. He
8. They   9. She
10. it   11. It
12. them   13. They
14. me   15. It
16. I   17. We
18. our

Page 45

2. 6:00 PM
3. 2 hours, 20 minutes
4. 2:50 PM
5. 3:00 PM; 7:00 PM
6. 10:50 PM

Page 46

1. Gather the ingredients.
2. Let the pie cool for at least 10 minutes before serving.
3. Grease the bottom of a large pie plate.
4. Test the pie for doneness by inserting a knife in the middle.
5. Yes. Reasons will vary. Instructions will vary.

Page 47

2. Circle: 10, 4, 5, 2, 1, 20; 6 factors
3. Circle: 7; 1 factor
4. Circle: 6, 9, 4, 12, 3; 5 factors
5. Circle: none; 0 factors
6. Circle: 25, 2, 100, 50, 10, 5, 20; 7 factors
7. Circle: 9, 6, 3, 18; 4 factors
8. Circle: 8, 4; 2 factors
Answer: A promise
9. Factors for 16: 8, 2, 16, 4, 1
10. Factors for 12: 2, 4, 12, 1, 6, 3
11. Factors for 28: 14, 7, 4, 2, 28, 1
12. Factors for 30: 10, 3, 30, 1, 6, 5, 15, 2

Page 48

Page 49

1. Multiply by 10		2. Multiply by 100		3. Multiply by 1,000	
Input	Output	Input	Output	Input	Output
2.05	20.5	.430	430	16.3	16,300
0.94	9.4	1.86	186	.089	89
25.42	254.2	50.09	5,009	8.51	8,510
7.48	74.8	.033	3.3	0.726	726

4. Multiply by 10		5. Multiply by 100		6. Multiply by 1,000	
Input	Output	Input	Output	Input	Output
3.905	39.05	0.001	.1	0.36	360
0.008	0.08	7.82	782	1.39	1,390
19.4	194	0.292	29.2	100.1	100,100
90.76	907.6	84.19	8,419	78.05	78,050

7. Multiply by 10		8. Multiply by 100		9. Multiply by 1,000	
Input	Output	Input	Output	Input	Output
0.15	1.5	0.355	35.5	545.01	545,501
27.18	271.8	7.22	722	.180	180
8.661	86.61	81.01	8,101	.014	14
.907	9.07	0.909	90.9	43.00	43,000

Page 50

Movie reviews will vary.

Page 51

1.
8	5	2	15
3	14	9	4
13	0	7	10
6	11	12	1

2.
16	6	3	5
5	15	10	4
11	1	8	14
2	12	13	3

3.
3	6	9	19
10	18	4	5
8	1	17	11
16	12	7	2

4.
10	7	4	16
5	18	11	6
17	2	9	12
8	13	16	3

5.
11	8	5	14
6	20	12	7
19	3	10	13
9	14	18	4

Page 52

2. children's   3. Women's
4. babies'   5. rats'
6. girls'   7. horses
8. students'   9. boxes'
10. grandma's   11. puppies'
12. ladies
Answer: A chick in an egg

Page 53

Tomatoes	Olives	Cheese
olives	cheese	mushrooms
cheese	mushrooms	bacon
mushrooms	bacon	chicken
bacon	chicken	onions
chicken	onions	egg
onions	egg	broccoli
egg	broccoli	sprouts
broccoli	sprouts	
sprouts		
Mushrooms	Bacon	Chicken
bacon	chicken	onions
chicken	onions	egg
onions	egg	broccoli
egg	broccoli	sprouts
broccoli	sprouts	
sprouts		
Onions	Egg	Broccoli
egg	broccoli	sprouts
broccoli	sprouts	
sprouts		

What is the total number of possible combinations? 45

Page 54

Descriptive adjectives will vary. Sentences will vary.

Page 55

2. Range: 27
Mode: 98
Median: 84
Mean: 87
3. Range: 51
Mode: 36
Median: 79
Mean: 71
4.

Stems	Leaves
3	2 4 6 6

4	2 8
5	0 5
8	1

Range: 49
Mode: 36
Median: 42
Mean: 46
5.

Stems	Leaves
6	2 5 6
7	3 5 9
8	4 7 7

Range: 25
Mode: 87
Median: 75
Mean: 75
6.

Stems	Leaves
1	5 8 9
2	0 2 5 5 7 9

Range: 14
Mode: 25
Median: 22
Mean: 22

Page 56

1. bold, brave, or adventurous; the family members live adventurous lives.
2. falling quickly; "He jumped out of windows" and "ten long stories to the ground."
3. Because they might not know what to do, so it's better to have someone with you.
4. impress or amaze; she sails off the jumps into the air and the crowd cheers
5.–6. Sentences will vary.

Page 57

2. 225
3. 25
4. Wednesday and Thursday
5. rise
6. 175

Page 58

2. c   3. b   4. d
5. a   6. b   7. c
8. b   9. d   10. a
11. b   12. d

Page 59

2. 64 ft.   3. 54 ft.
4. 48 sq. ft. 5. 50 sq. ft.
6. 40 sq. ft. 7. 60 sq. ft.
8. 334 ft.   9. 362 sq. ft.

Page 60

2. length   3. teeth
4. reptile   5. star
6. ocean   7. calves
8. hand   9. river
10. words   11. foot

12. baseball 13. England
14. grandma 15. Japanese
16. jungle 17. children
18. frog

Page 61
Aaron: painting
Ellie: swimming
Jake: hiking
Nicole: canoeing

Page 62
Letters will vary.

Page 63
2. $8.80
3. $9.35
4. $11.16
5. $15.20; $4.80
6. $10.65; $4.35
7. $13.05
8. $26.40

Page 64
2. wisdom
3. love
4. understanding
5. wealth
6. freedom
7. joy
8. intelligence
Answers will vary.

Page 65
2. 24 feet; 288 inches
3. 120 meters; 12,000 centimeters
4. 74 inches; 1.80 meters
5. 36,000 meters; 22.32 miles
6. 19.8 meters; 22 yards
7. 90 meters; 900 feet
8. Mando; 22.4 kilometers; 12.4 miles

Page 66
Sentences will vary.

Page 67
1. The Cheetahs won the game.
Final Score: Cheetahs 33, Mustangs 30
2. 38 yards; 42 yards
3. Cheetah 25 yard line; 50%
4. 151 yards
5. 70 yards; 7 first downs
6. Final Score: Cheetahs 39, Mustangs 40

Page 68
2. Jaguars and toucans live in the rain forest.
3. Tina, Shiki, and Sonya are talented dancers.
4. Blue whales and dolphins are mammals that live in the ocean.
5. Shells, starfish, and crabs are on the beach.
6. Cats are fun and lovable but can be difficult to train.
7. Cell phones are good for safety but can be annoying to people around you.
8. Red fire ants should be left alone or removed by a professional.
9. Daniel runs very fast but doesn't like football.
10. Trina lives in the mountains and grows all of her own food.

Page 69

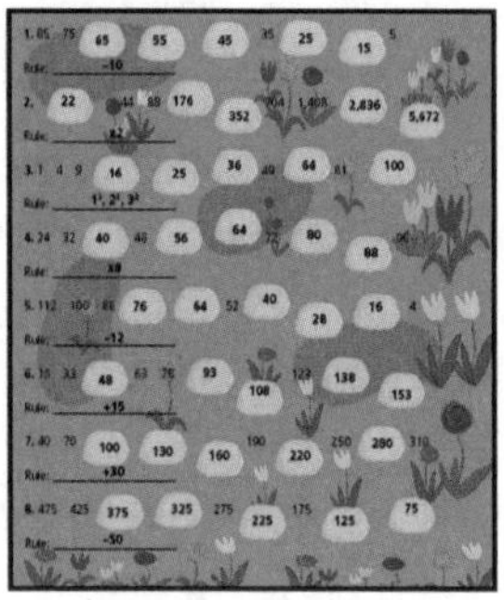

Page 70
1. surfing the tube
2. language or terms
3. drop in on someone else's wave
4. Any three: mullering, donut, eating it, pounding
5. goofy foot
6. happy or excited

Page 71
2. 55.05
3. 2.04
4. 9.035
5. 0.0003
6. 0.0085
7. .0127
8. 0.0006
9. 0.0058, .058, 0.580, 5.80, 58.0
10. 0.001, .010, 1.001, 10.01, 100.10
11. 0.0091, .0910, 9.001, 9.010, 9.910
12. 0.00537, 0.0537, 5.371, 53.07, 537.00

Page 72
2. expository 3. persuasive
4. descriptive 5. expository
6. narrative 7. persuasive
8. descriptive

Page 73
2. c 3. c 4. a
5. b 6. b 7. c
8. a

Page 74
Persuasive writing will vary.

Page 75

Double Chocolate Tower Cake		
1 Cake	**5 Cakes**	**8 Cakes**
1 cup butter, softened	5 cups	8 cups
1 Tbs. instant coffee	5 Tbs.	8 Tbs.
$1\frac{1}{3}$ cups water	$6\frac{2}{3}$ cups	$10\frac{2}{3}$ cups
8 oz. chocolate chips	40 oz.	64 oz.
5 eggs	25 eggs	40 eggs
2 tsp. vanilla	3 Tbs., 1 tsp.	5 Tbs., 1 tsp.
$2\frac{1}{4}$ cups flour	$11\frac{1}{4}$ cups	18 cups
$1\frac{1}{2}$ Tbs. baking powder	$7\frac{1}{2}$ Tbs.	12 Tbs.
$\frac{1}{2}$ tsp. salt	$2\frac{1}{2}$ tsp.	4 tsp.
$1\frac{1}{2}$ tsp. cinnamon	2 Tbs., $1\frac{1}{2}$ tsp.	4 Tbs.

Chocolate Fudge Icing		
1 Batch	**5 Batches**	**8 Batches**
$\frac{3}{4}$ cup heavy cream	3 cups	6 cups
6 oz. chocolate chips	30 oz.	48 oz.
$\frac{1}{4}$ tsp. vanilla	$1\frac{1}{4}$ tsp.	2 tsp.
3 cups powdered sugar	15 cups	24 cups
2 Tbs. milk	10 Tbs.	16 Tbs.

Page 76
2. <u>Mona Lisa</u>
3. "If I Had a Brontosaurus"
4. <u>Harry Potter and the Chamber of Secrets</u>
5. <u>Legends of the Hidden Temple</u>
6. "America the Beautiful"
7. <u>If I Were in Charge of the World and Other Worries</u>
8. <u>Los Angeles Times</u>
9. <u>Sports Illustrated for Kids</u>
10. "Lost in the Middle of the Night"
11. <u>Romeo and Juliet</u>
12. "How the Tiger Got Its Stripes"
13. "Ten Tricks to Teach Your Dog"
14. "Farmer in the Dell"
15. <u>Julie of the Wolves</u>
16. <u>The Road to Rock and Roll</u>
Sentences will vary.

Page 77
Kevin: beagles
Luke: poodles
Mira: labs
Tham: huskies
Raul: dalmations

Page 78
New words will vary.

Page 79
2. 24 boys
3. 38 boys and girls
4. 16 boys
5. basketball; soccer
6. 220 students

Page 80
1. Darkness filled my room like a thick blanket; The trees held onto their leaves like protective mothers.
2. friendly and greeting
3. show her cheery face
4. velvet veil, black
5. screeched and clattered; the branches against the house
6.–10. Sentences will vary.

Page 81
2. 77 – (13 x 3) = 38
3. 80 + (30 ÷ 2) = 95
4. 105 = 15 x (3 + 4)
5. 6 x (12 – 9) = 18
6. 16 + (19 – 18) = 17 or (16 + 19) – 18 = 17
7. (72 ÷ 8) x 8 = 72
8. (57 – 25) x 15 = 480
9. 50 = 20 + (6 x 5)
10. 29 – (21 ÷ 7) = 26
11. (98 ÷ 49) x 25 = 50
12. (106 x 2) ÷ 4 = 53

Page 82
Underline: Tigers are known around the world for their beauty, but they face an uncertain future.
Cross out: Rare albino tigers are white. You can see tigers in most zoos. Humans should try to save tigers.
Paragraphs will vary.

Page 83
2. $\frac{1}{6}$ 3. $\frac{13}{15}$
4. 24 tickets 5. 6 pieces
6. $\frac{1}{2}$ tank 7. $12\frac{1}{12}$
8. $3\frac{5}{12}$ 9. $\frac{5}{8}$
10. $8\frac{5}{16}$ 11. 4
12. $11\frac{1}{2}$

Page 84
Myths will vary.

Page 85
2. $\frac{2}{8}$ or $\frac{1}{4}$ 3. $\frac{2}{8}$ or $\frac{1}{4}$
4. $\frac{3}{30}$ or $\frac{1}{10}$ 5. $\frac{20}{30}$ or $\frac{2}{3}$
6. $\frac{7}{30}$ 7. $\frac{1}{6}$
8. $\frac{3}{6}$ or $\frac{1}{2}$ 9. $\frac{2}{6}$ or $\frac{1}{3}$

Page 86
2. glossary
3. newspaper
4. almanac
5. index
6. encyclopedia
7. newspaper
8. table of contents
9. index
10. phone book
11. almanac
12. atlas

Page 87
2. 3.75 3. 100
4. 26.4 5. 21
6. 225 7. 16.8
8. 455.6 9. 51.2
10. $1.25 11. $16.50
12. 4 students 13. 96 pitches
14. $134.40 15. $7.27

Page 88

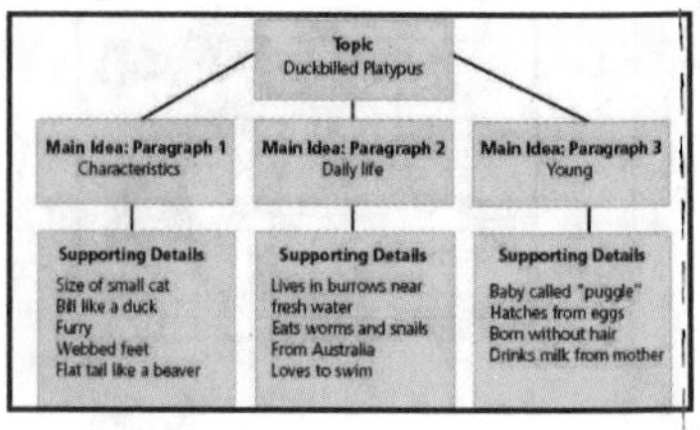

Page 89
2. 77,200 seats
3. $448
4. $110.00
5. 348,000 seats
6. $3,072,000
7. 108,550 seats
8. $2,700

Page 90
2. c 3. c 4. a
5. a 6. d 7. b
8. d 9. a 10. d

Page 91
1. 11
2. 6
3. 40; $n \div 4 = 10$
4. 4; $8n = 32$
5. 15; $n \div 3 = 5$
6. 18; $n + 48 = 66$

Page 92
1. To persuade people to travel
2. Possible answer: Traveling to different places and meeting new people can teach you a lot about the world. You can learn to appreciate a whole new world you never knew before!
3. Answers will vary.
4. The passage says that in each new place, I might see different animals and people. I might learn about the people who live there, including their history and art.
5. They might not learn to appreciate other countries and cultures.
6. Answers will vary.

Page 93

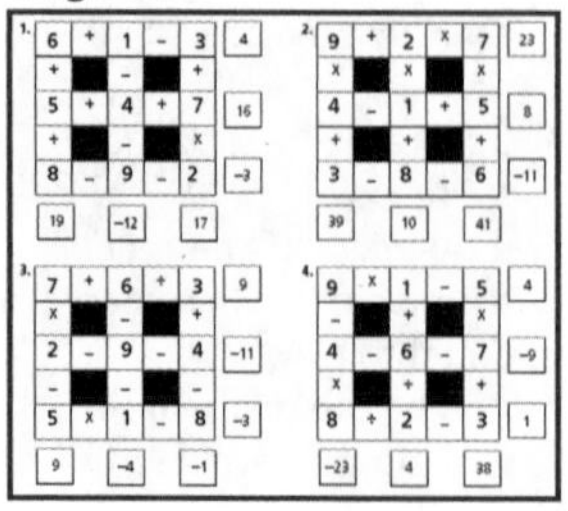